Habit

For Aristotle, excellence is not an act but a habit, and Hume regards habit as 'the great guide of life'. However, for Proust habit is problematic: 'if habit is a second nature, it prevents us from knowing our first.'

What is habit? Do habits turn us into machines or free us to do more creative things? Should religious faith be habitual? Does habit help or hinder the practice of philosophy? Why do Luther, Spinoza, Kant, Kierkegaard and Bergson all criticize habit? If habit is both a blessing and a curse, how can we live well in our habits?

In this thought-provoking book Clare Carlisle examines habit from a philosophical standpoint. Beginning with a lucid appraisal of habit's philosophical history she suggests that both receptivity and resistance to change are basic principles of habit formation. Carlisle shows how the philosophy of habit not only anticipates the discoveries of recent neuroscience but illuminates their ethical significance. She asks whether habit is a reliable form of knowledge by examining the contrasting interpretations of habitual thinking offered by Spinoza and Hume. She then turns to the role of habit in the good life, tracing Aristotle's legacy through the ideas of Joseph Butler, Hegel, and Félix Ravaisson, and assessing the ambivalent attitudes to habit expressed by Nietzsche and Proust.

She argues that a distinction between habit and practice helps to clarify this ambivalence, particularly in the context of habit and religion, where she examines both the theology of habit and the repetitions of religious life. She concludes by considering how philosophy itself is a practice of learning to live well with habit.

Clare Carlisle is Lecturer in Philosophy of Religion at King's College London. She is the author of three books on Kierkegaard, including *Kierkegaard's Philosophy of Becoming: Movements and Positions* (2005) and *Kierkegaard's Fear and Trembling* (2010). In 2008 she published the first English translation of Félix Ravaisson's seminal essay *De l'habitude*.

Thinking in Action

Series editors: Simon Critchley, *The New School University, USA*, and Richard Kearney, *Boston College, USA,* and *University College Dublin, Ireland*

Thinking in Action is a major new series that takes philosophy to its public. Each book in the series is written by a major international philosopher or thinker, engages with an important contemporary topic, and is clearly and accessibly written. The series informs and sharpens debate on issues as wide ranging as the Internet, religion, the problem of immigration and refugees, criticism, architecture, and the way we think about science. Punchy, short and stimulating, **Thinking in Action** is an indispensable starting point for anyone who wants to think seriously about major issues confronting us today.

CLARE CARLISLE

On
Habit

Routledge
Taylor & Francis Group

LONDON AND NEW YORK

First published 2014
by Routledge
2 Park Square, Milton Park, Abingdon, Oxon, OX14 4RN

And published by Routledge
711 Third Ave., New York City, NY 10017

Routledge is an imprint of the Taylor & Francis Group,
an informa business

British Library Cataloguing in Publication Data
A catalogue record for this book is available from the British Library

Library of Congress Cataloging in Publication Data
Carlisle, Clare, 1977–
    On habit/Clare Carlisle. – 1 [edition].
    pages cm. – (Thinking in action)
    Includes bibliographical references and index.
    1. Habit (Philosophy) I. Title.
    B105.H32C37 2014
    128'.4 – dc23   2013037770

ISBN: 978-0-415-61913-4 (hbk)
ISBN: 978-0-415-61914-1 (pbk)
ISBN: 978-0-203-81694-3 (ebk)

Typeset in Joanna and DIN
by Florence Production Ltd, Stoodleigh, Devon, UK

**For John
my brother in habit**

Contents

Acknowledgements

Thank you to all at Routledge who have made this book possible, especially Tony Bruce, Adam Johnson, and my series editor Simon Critchley. Thanks to King's College London – and to my colleagues in the Dean's Office, the Department of Theology and Religious Studies, and the Department of Philosophy – for providing a supportive, stimulating and fun environment in which to work. Another kind of support, even more indispensable, has been given by my friends at Sale, and by Russel most of all.

Several people have read and commented on drafts of this book. Simone Kotva, Simon Oliver and Dave Johnson provided particularly detailed and productive comments on the manuscript. Helpful feedback has also been gratefully received from John Callanan, Mark Sinclair, Don Cupitt and Mark Textor. The constructive criticism and generous encouragement offered by anonymous reviewers at early and late stages of the writing process have also been most welcome.

It has been a pleasure to write a book on a subject that has proved interesting and relevant to so many friends, students, acquaintances and strangers. Outside academic circles, mention of previous research projects has often been followed by awkward silence – but mention of a book on habit always invites good questions, thoughtful reflections or entertaining anecdotes. I have been fortunate to have been given many opportunities to speak and write about my research on habit, and this book has been enriched by discussions at seminars, colloquia, conferences, workshops and so on. But I am especially grateful to the good friends who have listened to, conversed with and argued against me as I have 'worked on' habit over the last few years. Among these are Mark Sinclair, Simon Oliver, George Pattison, Don Cupitt, Rupert Shortt, Tristram Stuart, Kate Wharton, David Wood, and John Tresch – to whom this book is dedicated.

'Let not habit do violence to you . . .'

Parmenides, 'On Nature'

'Rest and silence awaken.'

Ravaisson, Of Habit

One

BLESSING OR CURSE?

In 1799 the Académie des sciences in Paris announced an essay competition on the subject of habit. In the introduction to his prize-winning essay, Pierre Maine de Biran points out that his subject matter presents him with a peculiar task:

> Reflect on what is habitual! Who could or would wish to begin such reflection? How should one suspect some mystery in what one has always seen, done, or felt? About what should one inquire, should one be in doubt, should one be astonished? Heavy bodies fall, movement is communicated; the stars revolve over our heads; nature spreads out before our eyes her greatest phenomena: and what subject for wonder, what subject for inquiry could there be in such familiar things?[1]

Maine de Biran is referring here to the difficulty of reflecting on 'what is habitual' rather than on habit itself. Nevertheless, habit could be added to his list of the familiar things that we normally allow to go unnoticed. Habit is, quite literally, an everyday phenomenon. Each morning we are carried along by the force of habit – out of bed, to the bathroom, down the stairs, out to work – and each evening we are carried home again. As David Hume observes, 'custom, where it is strongest, not only covers our natural ignorance, but even conceals itself, and seems not to take place, merely because it is found in the highest degree.'[2]

Our tendency to overlook habit can be explained by one aspect of habit itself: the way in which familiarity and repetition dull our senses. Marcel Proust describes habit as a 'heavy curtain' which 'conceals from us almost the whole universe, and prevents us from knowing ourselves.'[3] Not only this: habit 'cuts off from things which we have witnessed a number of times the root of profound impression and of thought which gives them their real meaning.'[4] Proust realized that an artist has to draw back, or tear open, this curtain of habit, so that the most familiar features of our world become visible, meaningful, and cause for wonder. But this is also the philosopher's task. Although it is often said – quoting Plato or Aristotle – that philosophy begins with wonder, the wondering state of mind is only reached by first penetrating the heavy curtain of habit.[5]

So habit is a peculiarly philosophical issue, and it is also an important and profound feature of ordinary life. A few European philosophers have gone so far as to claim, like many teachers in the Buddhist tradition, that habit provides 'an answer to the problem of the self', that our continuing identity through time and change is produced by the tenacity of habit.[6] If this is true – and perhaps even if it is not quite true – then habit's elusiveness and obscurity belong to the mystery of human selfhood. The question of habit may be inseparable from our hardest, deepest, most insistent question: who *are* we? who *am* I?

In spite of the difficulty of reflecting on habit, most of our great philosophers have something interesting to say about it.

Often their views conflict with one another. Aristotle thinks that habit lies at the heart of moral life. Spinoza argues that it leads us astray and prevents us from perceiving the deep intelligibility of nature. Hume regards custom as 'the great guide of human life', since it helps to make our world orderly and predictable. Kant suggests that it undermines our innate moral worth, making us 'ridiculous' and machine-like. Hegel claims that habit liberates us, although it can also be a deadening force. Nietzsche compares long-lasting habit to 'a tyrant' – but, fearing that life without habit would be 'intolerable', he recommends cultivating a succession of 'brief habits'. And when we consider the history of European philosophy with the question of habit in mind, less prominent thinkers also come into the foreground: Joseph Butler, Thomas Reid and Félix Ravaisson, as well as Maine de Biran, have each made significant contributions to the philosophy of habit.

From this long tradition of enquiry into habit emerge two lines of interpretation. According to the first, habit is an obstacle to reflection and a threat to freedom. Insofar as we think and act out of habit, we are unable to know ourselves or reflect critically on the world, and so we are intellectually, morally, and spiritually impoverished. Habit is a degradation of life, reducing spontaneity and vitality to mechanical routine. Habit is the rut we get stuck in. It makes us bored with ourselves, and boring to others. According to the second interpretation, habit is an indispensable part of life: it not only brings order, consistency and comfort to our ever-changing experiences, but also allows us to be creative and free. On this view, habit is the living, dynamic embodiment of our intelligence and our desire. Habit underlies the distinctive character of every being, but shared habits bring individuals together into communities – and therefore habit forms the basis of ethical and religious life.

These two contrasting views even emerge in response to the question of the relationship between habit and philosophy. As Maine de Biran points out, habit can be an obstacle to reflection, and here he echoes many other philosophers who have struggled against the force of habit. In the fifth century BC Parmenides issued a warning that has resounded through our philosophical tradition: 'let not habit do violence to you in the empirical way of exercising an unseeing eye and a noisy ear and tongue, but decide by reason.'[7] Philosophical method can be understood as an instrument in this struggle, designed to free both the philosopher and his students from ingrained ways of thinking. Socrates' questioning, Descartes' doubt, Heidegger's idiosyncratic vocabulary, as well as all the bizarre thought experiments invented by philosophers, are ingenious techniques deployed in the war on habit. However, we might wonder how philosophy would be possible without habit – without, for example, the learnt linguistic conventions that facilitate communication, and the physical habits of writing or typing which can become an indispensable condition of thought. On a more metaphysical note, Ravaisson argues that reflection on habit helps to overcome certain dualisms that are commonly thought to have plagued Western thought – between the mind and the body, between freedom and nature. (Even if this kind of dualism is not so deeply entrenched in our philosophical tradition as is often claimed, many philosophers seem to have got into a habit of complaining about it.)

This essay will look more closely at these diverging views of habit, and explore a fundamental ambivalence and ambiguity that underlies them. If the philosophical tradition tends to divide itself on the question of habit, this is because of a duplicity within the matter itself. Habit is at once a blessing and a curse. In this respect it is akin to the Greek concept of the *pharmakon*, which is a drug that may be both a poison and a cure. Jacques Derrida has used this idea to explore the ambivalence of writing, but it is even more apt in the case of habit, whose comforting and anaesthetizing properties can bring it close to compulsion and addiction. Derrida's definition of writing in his essay 'Plato's Pharmacy' can apply equally to habit: 'to repeat without knowing.'[8]

The most interesting philosophers of habit are those who recognize its duplicity. Hegel is particularly willing to acknowledge habit's positive and negative aspects: 'Habit is often spoken of disparagingly and called lifeless, casual and particular. And it is true that the form of habit, like any other, is open to anything we happen to put into it; and it is the habit of living which brings on death, or, if quite abstract, is death itself: and yet habit is indispensable for the *existence* of all intellectual life in the individual.'[9] On the question of freedom, Hegel argues that 'the want of freedom in habit . . . strictly speaking arises only in the case of bad habits, or so far as habit is opposed by another purpose: whereas the habit of right and goodness is an embodiment of liberty.'[10] He also points out that 'habit and familiarity' are essential conditions of thinking, and thus of philosophy.[11] It is often under the influence of Hegel that contemporary philosophers comment on the ambivalence of habit.[12] However, Hegel is more concerned with analysing the concept of habit than with assessing its effects and implications in different spheres of life.

In the following chapters I will explore how the *pharmakon* of habit influences knowledge, ethics, religion, the practice of philosophy, and perhaps even nature itself. The European philosophical tradition has yielded so much interesting writing on habit that simply compiling the most significant sources would be a worthwhile exercise – and to some extent I will attempt this here, and consider how these texts on habit reflect the broader history of philosophy. But this book is not primarily a history of habit: my concern is more to order the ideas of other thinkers in a way that sets out the dialectic which unfolds from reflection on habit itself. And elements of the interpretation of habit developed here may contribute something new to the discourse on habit that can be drawn from our philosophical tradition. One of these elements is the discovery of a double principle of habit – receptivity and resistance to change – a principle that operates ethically as well as ontologically. Another is the guiding metaphor for habit introduced later in this chapter, which connects its various meanings across different contexts. Perhaps most importantly, clarifying the distinction between habit and practice helps us to understand why attention has a transformative effect on habit in all the spheres of human life examined in this essay.

DEFINING HABIT

Many of Plato's dialogues show that questions of the form 'what is X?' tend to lead not to a clear answer, but to the realization that concepts which we thought we understood are in fact complicated, slippery, and perhaps even impossible to define. In the case of habit there are additional difficulties: as Hegel puts it, 'We are accustomed to the idea of habit; none the less to determine the Notion of habit is hard.'[13] But it is important to ask the question 'what is habit?', if only to bring to light this concept's particular complexity and elusiveness.

When we attempt to define habit a series of d
come into view. First, there is a distinction betv
syncratic, individual habits and collective habits, or (
These are linked, of course, by the fact that hal
contagious: certain habits, like certain diseases, are passed
around between beings who encounter one another. In the
Republic Plato notes the connection between imitation (*mimesis*)
and habit: 'Have you never noticed how imitation, if long
continued from an early age, becomes part of a person's
nature, turns into habits of body, speech and mind?'[15] Second,
we can distinguish between active and passive habituation –
that is to say, between acquiring the habit of acting in a certain
way, and becoming accustomed to familiar sensations and
experiences. This distinction between active and passive habit
has led several thinkers, beginning with Joseph Butler, to
identify a 'double law' of habit, which will be considered at
some length in this essay. Third, habit can be either a source
or a result of actions. We sometimes say that we act 'out of
habit', implying that habit is a cause; but we can also recognize
that habits are themselves brought into being through the
repetition of an action or experience. Indeed, habit can be both
the source and the result of action, so that it is self-
perpetuating.[16] Fourth, there is an important distinction
between habit as an aptitude, skill or facility, and habit as a
tendency or inclination. Driving a car or riding a bicycle may
be entrenched habits in the sense that they are acquired
through repetition and can be executed without much thought
or attention, but this sort of habit is not usually compulsive,
and may be changed with little effort. By contrast, habitual
behaviours such as gestures and turns of phrase, nail-biting
and excessive consumption involve a tendency to act in a
certain way, and can be very difficult to restrain.

John Locke and Thomas Reid both propose definitions of habit that bring together these last two points. In his *Essay concerning Human Understanding* (1690), Locke states that habit is 'the power or ability in Man, of doing any thing, when it has been acquired by frequent doing the same thing', but he distinguishes this sense of habit from the idea of a 'disposition' – a form of habit that, like a coiled spring, is 'forward, and ready upon every occasion to break into Action.'[17] This distinction had not been recognized by Thomas Hobbes, who in 1655 defined habit as 'motion made more easy and ready by custom; that is to say, by perpetual endeavour, or by iterated endeavours.'[18] Ability, ease and readiness might be regarded as varying degrees of habit, but for Locke the difference between them is significant. He illustrates this by comparing two character traits: boldness, which is a 'power' to act or speak without fear; and 'testiness', which is an 'aptness to be angry'. While boldness is simply an acquired capacity which can be drawn on when the occasion requires it, testiness is, as Locke puts it, 'forward', apparently having its own momentum to 'break into Action' without prior reflection or decision.[19]

The first edition of the *Encyclopædia Britannica*, published in Edinburgh in 1771, equivocates between the two senses of habit distinguished by Locke. Here habit, considered as a philosophical term, is defined as 'an aptitude or disposition either of mind or body, acquired by a frequent repetition of the same act.'[20] Reid, however, argues that the difference between aptitude and disposition is philosophically significant. Writing in 1778, Reid – perhaps drawing on both Hobbes and Locke – acknowledges that 'Habit is commonly defined, *A facility of doing a thing, having done it frequently,*' but argues that 'the habits which may, with propriety, be called "principles of action" must give more than a facility, they must give an inclination or impulse to do the action; and that, in many cases, habits have this force, cannot be doubted.'[21] Reid thinks that habits only have a *causal* force when they involve a tendency or 'proneness' to perform the action in question, so that some effort is needed *not to act* thus. This qualification, he notes, departs from the way habit has been understood within the Aristotelian tradition:

> Aristotle makes wisdom, prudence, good sense, science and art, as well as the moral virtues and vices, to be *habits*. If he meant no more, by giving this name to all those intellectual and moral qualities, than that they are all strengthened and confirmed by repeated acts, this is undoubtedly true. I take the word in a less extensive sense when I consider habits as principles of action. I conceive it as a part of our constitution, that what we have been accustomed to do, we acquire, not only a facility, but a proneness to do so on like occasions; so that it requires a particular will and effort to forbear it, but to do it, requires very often no will at all. We are carried by habit as by a stream in swimming, if we make no resistance.[22]

The distinction highlighted by Reid perhaps underlies the contrasting evaluations of habit. If we regard habit as a skill or aptitude, then it appears quite harmless, and in many cases very helpful. But if, as Reid suggests, habit considered as a principle of action carries us along like the current of a stream, it has a force of its own that may well run counter to our rational decisions, and even to our desires. The examples of boldness and testiness offered by Locke do perhaps imply a normative distinction between habit as aptitude or skill, and habit as disposition or tendency – as if only bad habits have a spontaneous, 'forward' quality that makes them difficult to restrain. But just as skills can be used for good or ill, so tendencies may be virtuous or vicious.

As well as evoking a series of distinctions, the attempt to define habit raises some difficult metaphysical and epistemological questions. A habit is not an easily identifiable physical object. Indeed, it is not at all clear what kind of thing a habit is. We may certainly infer the presence of a habit when we observe repeated actions or patterns of behaviour. But can we tell the difference, as onlookers, between actions that are habitual, and those that are occasional and context-dependent? Can we actually *see* another's habit? We can perhaps gain a more immediate apprehension of habit in our own movements. This tends to happen as an exception rather than as a rule, for habits show themselves when they are disrupted. So, for example, you reach for your keys, or grope for the light switch – and before you've completed the movement you realize that it is redundant: you have given your keys to a guest who is waiting in for you; the light bulb still hasn't been changed. In such circumstances, the force of habit can be *caught in the act*, and recognized as such. But even so, we are becoming aware of a single impulse that signals the presence of a habit, and not the habit itself.

In either of these cases – the third-person or the first-person inference of a habit – what we infer is, as Reid suggests, an underlying principle of action. This might be regarded as a disposition or a tendency, which, we believe, causes the action in question, so that we say that someone *acts out of habit*. But does this 'disposition' or 'tendency' continue to exist when the habit is not being exercised?[23] How might it be detected? In what sense does a 'path of least resistance' *exist*, when it is not being taken? On this question, we might find recourse to the metaphysical concepts of potentiality and actuality. A tendency to act is not a distinct, stable object, but it is not nothing either: it is a *potentiality* that is actualized whenever the habitual actions are performed. However, potentiality and actuality are relative terms. Relative to action, a tendency is something potential rather than actual. But it is also true to say that something may or may not have the potential to acquire a certain kind of habit – so that, for example, a young child has the potential to ride a bike and to do maths, but a kitten does not have this potential. In this respect, a habit that has been acquired is something actual, in relation to the mere potentiality to acquire it. So habit is an actuality in one sense, but a potentiality in another. Habitual tendencies may share something in common with what Gilles Deleuze calls 'the virtual', which is as real as actuality, as dynamic as potentiality, and as myriad and shifting as possibility. All this perhaps goes some way towards clarifying the kind of thing habit is, and the kind of being it has, but also seems to raise further questions.

Repetition is another source of philosophical difficulty, since it implies both identity and difference and thus raises the perennial question of how these elemental concepts are connected. Hume points out that habits develop when repetition 'makes a difference', and this seems puzzling because in ordinary discourse repetition implies a recurrence of the same.[24] This familiar idea is, in turn, philosophically questionable: is anything *really* identical to anything else? And if anything remains identical through time, would it have to be disrupted in order to recur? In his enigmatic novella *Repetition* (1843) Søren Kierkegaard raises 'the question of repetition – whether or not it is possible': his narrator-pseudonym, Constantin Constantius, addresses this question experimentally by trying to repeat a fondly remembered trip to Berlin, but this fails disastrously, and Constantin concludes that 'repetition is too transcendent for me.'[25] More speculatively, however, he asserts that 'if God himself had not willed repetition' then the world would never have come into being, and that 'the world continues because it is a repetition.'[26] This turns on its head the more intuitive idea that repetition is the iteration of *something* – of an established identity. Kierkegaard's pseudonym suggests that, on the contrary, repetition constitutes the stable identity of something through time.

This obscure problematization of repetition is developed more systematically by Deleuze, who in *Difference and Repetition* (1962) argues that repetition is prior to identity or sameness, and not vice versa.[27] This suggests that identity is produced by habit, making habit a force that generates something new, rather than the effect of an established identity that seeks to conserve itself. The idea that repetition makes differences as well as identities leaves us with the rather paradoxical thought that through its repetition an entity makes a difference to itself. And this possibility has an ethical significance as well as a metaphysical one. As I repeat myself, how do I make a difference to myself? As we repeat ourselves, how do we make a difference to the world? As the world repeats itself, does it make a difference to God?

Our concept of habit is further complicated by the use of this English word to translate different Greek and Latin terms. In Aristotle's *Nicomachean Ethics*, for example, moral virtue is connected with both *ethos* and *hexis*. While *ethos* signifies character, custom, or way of life, a *hexis* is a disposition, capacity or tendency in the sense (or senses) outlined above. In Latin, *consuetudo* and *habitus* have similar meanings to *ethos* and *hexis* – and as we shall see in Chapter 3, some philosophers have drawn a sharp distinction between them. However, both pairs of terms are often translated into English by 'habit'.

These questions, distinctions and qualifications associated with the concept of habit indicate its complexity, and some of the points raised briefly here will be considered in more detail over the coming pages. We may not yet be able to say what habit is. Nevertheless, we all know how to use the word 'habit' — and reflection on this use offers another way to examine the concept of habit.

THE FORM OF NATURE

When we look at the various uses of the English word 'habit', we find a small family of concepts with a surprisingly large scope of reference. Understood as a settled tendency or disposition to behave in a particular way, 'habit' can be animal, vegetal or mineral. In mineralogy, 'habit' is a technical term for the way crystals are formed, and similarly in botany 'habit' describes the manner of a plant's growth — whether it shoots upwards, climbs, or creeps along the ground, for example. When applied to an animal, 'habit' signifies a pattern of behaviour — its ways of finding shelter, hunting, storing food, resting, mating, and so on. Within the human sphere, the term can be extended to include more complex and sophisticated kinds of activity, such as psychological patterns of thought and desire. It can also, however, denote a purely outward, physical way of being: a bearing, a posture, a demeanour, a way of holding oneself. This kind of habit is both subtle and powerful: it is possible to recognize a casual acquaintance from a distance, and from behind, simply by her gait or the incline of her head. Habit has also been used to mean a uniform, or a standard mode of dress — a riding habit, for example – although nowadays this usage tends to be confined to the robes worn by monks and nuns. The connection between habit and clothing is also apparent in the English words 'custom' and 'costume', and the French *coutume* and *couture*, which share a common root in *consuetudo*.

These uses have in common the idea of shape or form. A habit is a form that is distinctive to the individual in question, whether this is a rhododendron or a butterfly, a hedgehog or a horse rider. Several points arise from this basic observation. Habit can distinguish one group or species from another, or one individual from another. A habit of growth, amongst other features, distinguishes the rhododendron from the clematis, and similarly a habit of migration distinguishes one species of bird from another. But in the case of those organisms which have managed to flourish within and adapt to different environments, habits are more specific to breeds, tribes and communities. In the human sphere, of course, individuals even of the same family can have very different habits: here, habit is an effective way of distinguishing between two grey-haired, elderly, beige-coated neighbours as they shuffle or stride past one's window.

It seems, then, that although the concept of habit applies to a very broad range of beings, habit itself develops in the case of more sophisticated and highly functioning animals. In humans, this development encompasses cultural forms of expression such as the use of language and complex signs, and highly specialized forms of activity – baking a cake, driving a bus, programming a computer, conducting a scientific experiment, or presenting an academic paper. But furthermore, habit in the human domain diversifies into addiction, routine, skill, idiosyncratic behaviour, collective custom, and even explicit social practice that is deliberately conserved and handed on from one generation to the next. And, crucially, in human beings habit becomes reflective – that is to say, both an instrument and an object of reflection.

Habit lies at an indeterminate transition point between nature and culture within the human being. Humans share with plants the vegetal functions of growth, nutrition and generation; with simple animals the functions of breathing and digestion; and with more developed animals the functions of communication, social organization, and care and education of their young. And, of course, humans have their own distinctive forms of consciousness and expression which they pass on to one another.

The idea that human habit constitutes a transition from nature to culture is discussed by Hegel in his *Philosophy of Spirit*. In fact, habit appears at decisive points throughout Hegel's philosophical system: in his *Philosophy of Nature* he takes up the analysis of habit presented by the young French biologist Xavier Bichat in his pioneering *Recherches physiologiques sur la vie et la mort*; and in his *Philosophy of Right* Hegel considers the ethical and political significance of habit. In the *Philosophy of Spirit*, however, he embarks on a more technical analysis of habit, considered as a principle of human nature. In this text, habit is located in the passage from merely natural, organic life to a spiritual kind of existence – the emergence of a self. With habit comes a degree of freedom. On this point, Hegel echoes the insights of another French physiologist, Claude Perrault, who noted in 1680 that because habit 'has the power to make easy the exercise of all [the body's] internal functions', it allows the soul 'freedom to attend to those which are external'.[28] But Hegel also finds that habit facilitates a relation of ownership to sensations and other features of our experience. Through habit, he writes, 'the soul has the contents [of its experience] in possession, and contains them in such a manner that in these features it is not sentient, nor does it stand in relationship with them as distinguishing itself from them, nor is it absorbed in them, but has them and moves in them, without feeling or consciousness of the fact.'[29]

In *De natura deorum* Cicero writes that 'we seek with our human hands to create a second nature in the natural world,'[30] and Hegel suggests that this concept of 'second nature' expresses an equivocation on the naturalness of habit:

> Habit is rightly called a second nature; nature, because it is an immediate being of the soul; a second nature, because it is an immediacy created by the soul . . . In habit the human being's mode of existence is 'natural', and for that reason not free; but still free, so far as the merely natural phase of feeling is by habit reduced to a mere being of *his*, and he is no longer involuntarily attracted or repelled by it, and so no longer interested, occupied or dependent with regard to it.[31]

This contrasts with the Romantic idea that 'nature' has a spontaneity and a creative power that habit reduces to mechanical uniformity, rather as a child's spontaneity is progressively curbed by the imposition of social custom and convention. From this Romantic perspective a 'second nature' appears to corrupt or constrict what is truly natural, whereas for Hegel it is the elevation and fulfilment of nature.[32]

Underlying the various uses of the word 'habit', then, are hints about the significance of habit both throughout nature as a whole, and within human life. Habit might very broadly be defined as a particular way of being – that is to say, a distinctive form or style or posture of living. Habit is a principle of nature, albeit one that pushes beyond the boundaries of the natural, and so tests the distinction between nature and culture or artifice. Habit can normalize the artificial, and make what is natural strange and uncomfortable. This is exemplified by the woman who is so used to wearing make-up that she feels unable to leave the house 'without my face on'; similarly, our collective caffeine habit makes a day without tea or coffee seem unthinkable. Such modifications become a 'second nature' that allows us to function 'as normal', and in this respect they differ only in degree from the habit of a heroin addict who becomes ill when he is deprived of his drugs. Through habit, nature both forms and re-forms itself, lets itself be cultivated and constructed in a secondary way. But much more needs to be said about this conception of habit. Considered purely as a principle – that is to say, regardless of its scope and application, and the history of its use – what does habit consist in?

CONSTANCY AND CHANGE

The principle of habit involves both constancy and change. On the one hand, it is through habit that beings – whether human, animal, vegetal or mineral – hold their shape through time; they remain the same (or approximately the same) even in movement, for they repeatedly follow certain patterns and sequences. In this way, habit forms part of an individual's stable identity – and it may even constitute this identity. On the other hand, we can acquire habits only because we are changed by our actions and experiences. Habits develop when a repeated change, such as a movement or a sensation, makes a difference to a being's constitution. But, again, the changes that happen in habit acquisition produce an inclination to repeat, strengthen a conservative force, deepen a tendency to stay the same. Habit does not just involve both constancy and change: it *combines* constancy and change.

Ravaisson emphasizes this point at the beginning of his 1838 essay *De l'habitude*. 'Permanence and change are the first conditions of habit', he writes here, and he goes on to describe the kind of change involved in the development of a habit:

> Habit implies more than mere mutability; it does not simply imply mutability in something that remains without changing; it supposes a change in the disposition, in the potential, in the internal virtue of that in which the change occurs . . . From the lowest level of life, it seems that the continuity or repetition of a change modifies, relative to this change itself, the disposition of a being, and in this way modifies nature.[33]

Ravaisson illustrates this idea with an example taken from Aristotle's *Eudemian Ethics*: a stone, however many times it is thrown into the air, will not acquire a habit of ascending.[34] Stones are mutable – they can be corroded, split, or sculpted into different shapes – but, unlike living beings, they do not have a nature (or, as Ravaisson puts it, a disposition, potential or internal virtue) that can be modified.

Constancy and change are, then, the two basic aspects of habit. The etymology of habit seems to favour its invariable face: our English word can be traced to the Greek *ekhein* and the Latin *habere*, which both mean 'to have' and 'to hold'. As we have seen, the idea of holding carries the sense of an enduring posture, a way of holding oneself, that brings together diverse uses and applications of the concept of habit.

And the bare notion of having can be developed into more sophisticated concepts of possession and ownership, which again convey a relationship that is stable and continuous through time. Our *habitat*, after all, is the place to which we belong, and in which we keep our belongings.

In fact, the privileging of constancy rather than change in the linguistic origins of the concept of habit is highly significant within the philosophical tradition. As with so many philosophical concepts, the Greek *hexis* (from *ekhein*) – which became the Latin *habitus* (from *habere*) – came to birth in Aristotle's work, although it was prefigured by a less precise and systematic treatment in Plato.[35] In his *Categories* Aristotle defines *hexis* as an enduring quality, contrasting it with the term *diathesis*, which signifies a more ephemeral state.[36] A *hexis*, for example, might be the hardness of stone, the brittleness of glass, or the courage of a soldier, while a *diathesis* might be a transient quality of coolness or fatigue. In his study of ethical life, where the concept of *hexis* becomes most productive, Aristotle emphasizes that moral virtue involves the cultivation of long-lasting character traits. 'Having' or 'possessing' certain virtues amounts to a stable identity, so that *having* a capacity or a tendency to act with, for example, generosity or wisdom, signifies that a person *is* generous or wise. And likewise, in the case of vices, one who frequently runs from challenging situations *is* a coward, and a habitual heavy drinker *is* an alcoholic. 'One swallow does not make spring, nor one fine day', remarks Aristotle in the *Nicomachean Ethics*; 'Neither does one day or a short time make someone blessed and happy.'[37] In other words, the good life involves the sedimentation of actions, through repetition, into habits that come to constitute an abiding way of being.

Of course, the stable having and holding expressed in the concept of *hexis* need not be static. Habit's constancy might rest on a pattern of growth or of movement – as in the case of botanical or animal habit. And it incorporates variations and alterations within its general pattern. In any particular case, resistance to change is itself an *acquired* tendency, since it resists in a particular way, according to a particular pattern of action and experience – and it therefore testifies to an underlying capacity to be changed and formed. Still, this *hexis* aspect of habit emphasizes that repetition is a conservative force that, secured by a fundamental inertia, produces consistency and identity. It is as if mere repetition of an action or encounter – however blind, accidental or meaningless – imposes a command, an order, a rule, which is assimilated by the organism and becomes its own internal order, its self-regulation. This rule of habit may well run counter to a rational or a moral order.

The other aspect of habit prioritizes a more radical kind of change. While habit's conservative face expresses resistance to change, its open face expresses receptivity to change. As Aristotle's example of the stone illustrates, only beings which have an impressionable nature are capable of contracting habits. Only in such beings can repetition generate – or erode – a disposition. Habit implies responsiveness to the environment. We might say that habit implies subjectivity, provided that this can be understood, very broadly, as signifying sensitivity without necessarily requiring consciousness, so that it encompasses plants and very simple organisms. Deleuze writes that 'a soul must be attributed to the heart, to the muscles, nerves and cells, but a contemplative soul whose entire function is to contract a habit.'[38] Of course, the phenomenon of habit also shows us that we are receptive to the changes incurred by our own actions and decisions. In habit we not only yield to external influence: we are inescapably receptive to ourselves, formed as the (often unintended) consequence of our movements.

Just as the resistance to change implicit in habit contains within it an element of flexibility and variation – and, as an acquired mode of resistance, testifies to our receptivity to change – so receptivity has its own limit. This points to the important distinction between plasticity and flexibility, fluidity or amorphousness.[39] If we were simply receptive to change, without limit, then we would be incapable of habit. Each new action or experience would transform us, so that we would have no character or integrity to call our own. We would be empty, entirely subject to circumstance, blown hither and thither by the winds of change. Neither absolute resistance nor absolute receptivity allow a thing to have a *nature*. The idea of plasticity, on the other hand, captures the twin conditions of habit in bringing together both resistance and receptivity to change. Materials that are plastic can hold their form as well as take on a new form.

Towards the end of the nineteenth century William James proposed an elegant definition of plasticity as 'the possession of a structure weak enough to yield to an influence, but strong enough not to yield all at once.' Insisting on the materiality of habit, James argues that 'organic matter, especially nervous tissue, seems endowed with a very extraordinary degree of plasticity of this sort; so that we may without hesitation lay down [the principle] that *the phenomena of habit in living beings are due to the plasticity of the organic materials of which their bodies are composed.*'[40] In the 1930s the Canadian neurologist Donald Holding Hebb developed this insight through a series of experimental observations that called into question the

Pavlovian model of conditioning. Hebb argued that brain synapses are 'plastic', and a few years later Jerzy Konorski used the term 'plasticity' in a neurological context for the first time.[41] These ideas have come to dominate mainstream science: Ann Graybiel's summary of research on habit in neuroscience and psychology, published in 2008, emphasizes 'experience-dependent plasticity' and 'dynamically changing activity patterns' involving several different areas of the brain.[42] Indeed, recent years have seen a proliferation of popular books announcing a revolution in brain science: the discovery of 'the plastic mind', or 'the brain that changes itself', is seen as heralding a new materialism that marks a radical break with mechanistic ways of understanding the brain as a fixed or 'hard-wired' system.[43]

In fact, the neuroscientific concept of plasticity has much in common with far older concepts of disposition, habit and tendency, and even *hexis* itself. These philosophical concepts, particularly when they imply the metaphysical distinction between potentiality and actuality, already call into question mechanistic accounts of nature. (It would, after all, be silly to ascribe to a machine a disposition, habit or tendency to operate in a certain way.) So while contemporary accounts of the brain's plasticity help us to understand the processes of habit formation, philosophical reflection on habit helps us to understand the significance of plasticity. As we shall see in the following chapters, philosophers have explored and argued about the influence of habit on intellectual inquiry, moral life, and religious belief and practice. These discussions illuminate the modern idea of plasticity, enabling us to approach it not just as a scientific concept, but as a principle with ontological, epistemological, ethical and political implications.

Various metaphors have been proposed for habit: an iron chain (Augustine), a schoolmistress (Montaigne), a curtain and a veil (Proust), a spiral (Ravaisson), and a flowing stream (Reid). But reflection on the link between habit and plasticity draws attention to a particularly powerful metaphor: the pathway. This image brings together the two senses of habit distinguished by Locke and Reid – aptitude and tendency – for a pathway both facilitates a journey across rough terrain, and inclines us to take a particular route. Of course, we should not assume that a path is straight or linear. We shall see that certain philosophical reflections on habit suggest that its pathway is undulating, like the hills, or spiralling, like a coiled spring which repeatedly circles back upon itself to produce a forward momentum.

The constant and dynamic faces of habit are held together in the metaphor of a pathway. A pathway is both created and maintained by repeated movements – by sheep walking across moorland, for example. Yet pathways endure through the periods between these movements, although they will disappear if they fall out of use for too long. The formation of pathways also illustrates the idea that nature is modified (or, perhaps, modifies itself) through habit: the changes in a landscape mark a meeting point between what is natural and what is cultivated. And habit's dual principle of receptivity and resistance to change is exemplified by the conditions under which paths are created by movements through the land. In his 2012 book on pathways and landscape, Robert Macfarlane observes that 'the two main surfaces of the Western Isles – black peat and pale gneiss – are differently hostile to paths,' for the spongy peat swallows paths while the tough gneiss refuses them. This explains the practice of signing the way across such ground with cairns. Limestone, by contrast, is soft enough to be marked by raindrops yet resilient enough to hold these marks: 'Humans and animals, seeking a route, are guided by the pre-configured habits of the terrain. These pedestrians create preferential pathways, which in turn attract the flow of subsequent pedestrians, all of which etch the track of their passage with their feet as they go. In this way the path of a raindrop hundreds of thousands of years ago may determine the route of a modern-day walker.'[44]

Furthermore, the pathway metaphor indicates the broad scope of the concept of habit. It is not just that different sorts of beings – animals, vegetables and minerals – can acquire habits. Pathways run through the land, marking and guiding the movements of animals, but, according to the terminology of contemporary neuroscience, they also run between neurons in the brain. So habits can be both collective and individual phenomena. In both cases, pathways testify to plasticity: to resistance and receptivity to change, the dual principle of habit.

Philosophers intuited this principle long before the scientific discovery of the plastic mind. Where modern scientists speak of synapses (from the Greek *sunapsis*, meaning joint or connection), or neural pathways, early modern philosophers spoke of the pathways of 'animal spirits'.[45] In his *Search after Truth* (1674), Nicolas Malebranche argues that habits are formed through the connection of 'traces' within the brain: 'it is enough that many traces were produced at the same time for them all to arise again together. This is because the animal spirits, finding the path of all the traces made at the same time half open, continue on them since it is easier for them to travel those paths than through other parts of the brain.'[46] Malebranche suggests that the development of pathways eases the difficulties at first encountered in learning to speak a new language or play a musical instrument. He explains that pathways are opened and strengthened gradually, through repetition: 'little by little the animal spirits open and smooth these paths by their continual flow, so that in time they find no more resistance . . . when the spirits have passed through these traces many times, they enter there more easily than other places.'[47] A generation later, Locke echoes Malebranche in hypothesizing that habits of thinking, willing and bodily movement 'all seem to be but Trains of Motions in the Animal Spirits, which once set a going continue on in the same steps they have been used to, which by often treading are worn into a smooth path, and the Motion in it becomes easy and as it were Natural.'[48]

The pathway metaphor also conveys a sense of the temporality of habit. As Malebranche suggests, a path preserves traces of the activity by which it was formed. Each neural pathway, like a forest trail or a moorland track, is 'an archive of past habits and practices'.[49] Habit makes us historical beings – and in this respect it is very different from memory. If memory is an image of the past, habit is the past's repetition in the present. Our habits are not souvenirs, but the living embodiment of our history.[50] Habit is a forgetful appropriation and retention of the past: the dark, vibrant underside of memory.

Just as someone walking along a path can see the way ahead as well as the route already taken, so the temporality of habit reaches out towards the future as well as back into the past. Regarded simply as an ability or capacity, habit constitutes a potentiality to act in a certain way in the future. But considered as a tendency, habit is, as Locke observed, 'forward': it *anticipates* the future. Habits of association create an expectation that future events will follow a similar course, while habits of action, as we have seen, have a momentum of their own that propels a person along her well-travelled path. Ravaisson, drawing on Hume's analysis of habit, emphasizes this orientation to the future: an action that is repeated 'becomes more of a tendency, an inclination that no longer awaits the commandments of the will but rather anticipates them.'[51] Habit's anticipation of the future differs from imagination, just as its appropriation of the past differs from memory. Habit does not have to conjure an image of the future: we do not *look forward to* brushing our teeth in the evening, for we simply reach for the toothbrush when bedtime comes. Ravaisson describes this unreflective expectancy of habit as 'obscure': 'Continuity or repetition brings about a sort of obscure activity that increasingly anticipates both the impression of external objects in sensibility, and the will in activity.'[52] Through habit, then, temporality is shaped in a distinctive way, in the sense that the past and the future become one's own. Indeed, the 'having' of habit accomplishes an appropriation of time itself: while inert things like stones are simply *in time*, beings which are capable of habit *have a life-time*. As Ravaisson puts it, 'every living being has its own path'.[53]

The pathway, then, provides an enduring metaphor that reveals something about habit's genesis, effects and significance. If life is routinely envisaged as a journey, the pathway symbolizes the ambivalence of habit. As the 'great guide of human life', the path of habit facilitates our progress, and also leaves us free to enjoy the view or engage in conversation while walking through difficult terrain. But the ease of following a pathway without thinking or knowing where we are going may not be entirely to our advantage. Reliance on a well-trodden route discourages exploration of less familiar places, while an adventurous diversion may reward us with delightful new vistas – or it might lead to disaster.

THE DOUBLE LAW OF HABIT

There are many philosophical accounts and interpretations of habit, and some of them will be considered in detail in the chapters to follow. But one especially significant idea deserves to be examined here, since it is a development of the principle of habit. Ravaisson calls this 'the double law of habit', but it was first noted by Joseph Butler in his 1736 book *The Analogy of Religion, Natural and Revealed, to the Constitution and Course of Nature.* As this title suggests, Butler – an Anglican bishop – proposes a naturalistic interpretation of religion, largely in response to Hobbes's reductive, amoral naturalism. In his discussions of Christian morality Butler draws on Aristotle's virtue ethics, which as we have seen involves the concept of *hexis*. However, Butler supplements the Aristotelian account of virtue with his own analysis of the distinction between active and passive habit.

Butler observes that repetition has contrasting effects on actions and movements on the one hand, and sensations and feelings on the other. 'Passive habit loses in power by repetition, active gains', he states.[54] Butler was not the first person to point out that when we become accustomed to certain sensations we cease to notice them, or that repeated actions become easier and more assured. But he seems to have been the first philosopher to reflect on how these two phenomena come together. Since actions are often prompted or motivated by feelings and sensations, the active and passive aspects of habit combine to produce a more complicated effect:

From these two observations together; that practical [i.e. active] habits are formed and strengthened by repeated acts, and that passive impressions grow weaker by being repeated upon us; it must follow, that active habits may be gradually forming and strengthening, by a course of acting upon such and such motives and excitements, whilst these motives and excitements themselves are, by proportionable degrees, growing less sensible, i.e. are continually less and less sensibly felt, even as the active habits strengthen.[55]

These remarks on habit are offered within a discussion of 'moral discipline and improvement', and Butler's illustrations of his point reflect this context: he discusses how frequent exposure to danger or to distress can go together with increasingly courageous or compassionate actions. We will return to Butler's account of moral habit in Chapter 3, but what is important here is his development of the principle of habit in drawing attention to its dual effects.

Other eighteenth-century thinkers took up Butler's basic insight, but recognized that it is not restricted to the sphere of ethical practice. In his *Treatise of Human Nature* (1739), Hume tries to explain the fact that 'custom encreases all *active* habits, but diminishes *passive*.'[56] He suggests that new actions or ideas resist and agitate the flow of 'animal spirits' through the body and mind, and that frequent repetition erodes this resistance, 'produces a facility', and allows the spirits to settle into an 'orderly motion'.[57] And Bichat, in his 1799 *Recherches physiologiques sur la vie et la mort*, examines the dual effects of habit on judgement. Bichat finds that habit 'acts in an inverse ratio' upon feeling (*le sentiment*) and judgement, for 'feeling is constantly blunted by [habit], whereas judgement on the contrary owes to it its perfection. The more we look at an object, the less we are sensible of its painful or agreeable qualities and the better we judge all its attributes.'[58] Bichat suggests that whenever a sensation arises the mind automatically compares it with previous sensations, and that it is the *difference* between one sensation and another that we feel. New and unfamiliar sensations are therefore intense, and occupy our attention, but this effect is lessened by frequent repetition: 'every time we see an object, hear a sound, or taste a dish, etc., we find less difference between what we experience and what we have experienced . . . Every state of relative pleasure or pain is incessantly brought to a state of indifference by the influence of habit.'[59] But as feeling weakens, the activity of judging improves. Bichat illustrates this with the example of a man walking through a meadow full of flowers of different kinds: at first he is 'distracted' and absorbed by the mixture of scents, but as habit lessens and eventually effaces this initial feeling he is able to distinguish the particular smells of each plant, and to make judgements about them. According to Bichat, then, the two influences of habit may seem to be contrary, but in fact one explains the other. The diminution of sensation makes judgement easier, and in this way habit achieves the 'perfection of every act of animal life'.[60]

The distinction between activity and passivity is central to the nineteenth-century essays on habit by Maine de Biran and Ravaisson. Maine de Biran offers a clear statement of the two effects of habit: 'sensation, continued or repeated, fades, is gradually obscured and ends by disappearing without leaving any trace. Repeated movement gradually becomes more precise, more prompt, and easier.'[61] He disagrees with Bichat about the cause of these two effects, and he examines in much greater detail how they combine when our movements and feelings come together. In making a movement, he points out, we are both active and passive: we decide to move, but we also *are moved*, and every movement requires an effort, which we apprehend as a sensation. In other words, we cannot move without feeling our movements happen in our own bodies. Maine de Biran argues that this meeting point between activity and passivity is the origin of self-consciousness. Ravaisson follows this analysis very closely, but he identifies the contrary effects described by Maine de Biran as a unified 'double law of habit'.[62] Furthermore, he claims that this law can be explained by a single principle. According to Ravaisson, repetition weakens sensation and strengthens movement 'in the same way, by one and the same cause': the gradual development of an unreflective 'spontaneity', 'tendency' or 'desire'.[63]

Just as Hume broadens the application of Butler's 'double law' from the moral domain to habit in general, so Ravaisson develops Maine de Biran's analysis of habit within *la faculté de penser* by applying it to different domains – including moral and religious life, thus returning to Butler's original insights.[64] But what is especially interesting in Maine de Biran's study is how his reflection on the double law of habit leads to an ambivalent evaluation of its influence. He remarks that habit is the 'general cause of our progress on the one hand, of our blindness on the other. . . . It is to habit that we owe the facility, the precision, and the extreme rapidity of our movements and voluntary operations; but it is habit also which hides from us their nature and quantity.'[65]

An account of habit's *pharmakon*-like duplicity thus developed during the century of discourse on habit stretching from Butler to Ravaisson, and from Britain to France. Because sensations fade when they are repeated, familiarity can breed contempt – but it also brings comfort and ease. In habit, both pleasure and pain are reduced, and even brought to a point of neutrality. Because actions are strengthened by repetition, habit increases the efficiency and accuracy of our movements – but this same strengthening can be a problem when we want to change habits that have become deeply entrenched. And in human life, the combination of activity and passivity in the complex flow of experience, action, and interaction makes the duplicity of habit equally complex. This raises the question of whether it is possible to distil the liberating and therapeutic power of habit from its naturally duplicitous composition. Could we ever enjoy the benefits of this *pharmakon* without its damaging side effects?

NOTES

1 Pierre Maine de Biran, *The Influence of Habit on the Faculty of Thinking*, trans. Margaret Donaldson Boehm (Westport, CT: Greenwood Press, 1970), p. 47.

2 David Hume, *An Enquiry concerning Human Understanding*, in *Enquiries concerning Human Understanding and Concerning the Principles of Morals*, 3rd edn, ed. L. A. Selby-Bigge and P. H. Nidditch (Oxford: Clarendon Press, 1975), pp. 28–29 (IV.i).

3 Marcel Proust, *The Captive/The Fugitive*, vol. 5 of *In Search of Lost Time*, trans. C. K. Scott Moncrieff and Terence Kilmartin, revised by D. J. Enright (London: Vintage, 1996), p. 621.

4 Proust, *In Search of Lost Time*, vol. 6: *Time Regained*, p. 82.

5 See Plato, *Theaetetus*, trans. Benjamin Jowett, 155d: 'wonder is the feeling of a philosopher'. Aristotle echoes this in *Metaphysics* 982b 12: 'It is through wonder that men now begin and originally began to philosophize' (trans. Hugh Tredennick, Loeb Classical Library edition, Cambridge, MA: Harvard University Press, 1933).

6 Deleuze attributes this view to Hume: see Gilles Deleuze, *Empiricism and Subjectivity*, trans. Constantin V. Boundas (New York: Columbia University Press, 1991), p. x. On habit and identity in the Buddhist tradition, see

Clare Carlisle, 'Becoming and Unbecoming: The Theory and Practice of *Anatta*', *Contemporary Buddhism* 7, no. 1 (2006): 75–89; and on habit and identity more generally, see 'Creatures of Habit: The Problem and the Practice of Liberation', *Continental Philosophy Review* 38, nos. 1–2 (2006): 19–39.

7 A. H. Coxon (ed.), *The Fragments of Parmenides* (Assen/Maastricht: Van Gorcum, 1986), p. 58.

8 Jacques Derrida, *Dissemination*, trans. Barbara Johnson (Chicago: University of Chicago Press, 1983), p. 75.

9 *Hegel's Philosophy of Mind (Part Three of the Encyclopaedia of the Philosophical Sciences)*, trans. William Wallace and A. C. Miller (Oxford: Clarendon Press, 1971), p. 143 (§410).

10 Ibid., p. 141 (§410).

11 Ibid.

12 See Cathérine Malabou, 'Addiction and Grace', preface to *Of Habit*, by Félix Ravaisson, trans. Clare Carlisle and Mark Sinclair (London: Continuum, 2008), pp. vii–xx; Markus Gabriel and Slavoj Žižek, *Mythology, Madness and Laughter: Subjectivity in German Idealism* (London: Continuum, 2009), pp. 95–121.

13 *Hegel's Philosophy of Mind*, p. 143 (§410, *Zusatz*).

14 On the distinction between habit and custom, see Tom Crook, 'Habit as Switchpoint', *Body & Society* 19, nos. 2 and 3 (2013): 275–81.

15 Plato, *Republic*, trans. Tom Griffith, ed. G. R. F. Ferrari (Cambridge: Cambridge University Press, 2000), p. 84 (395c–d). In the early twentieth century, psychologists such as Gabriel Tarde and William McDougall drew on concepts of mimesis and repetition to develop theories of group psychology: see G. Tarde, *The Laws of Imitation* (London: Henry Holt & Co., 1903); W. McDougall, *An Introduction to Social Psychology* (London: Methuen, 1910). For an overview, see Lisa Blackman, 'Habit and Affect: Revitalizing a Forgotten History', *Body & Society* 19, nos. 2 and 3 (2013): 186–216.

16 For a detailed analysis of habit in relation to the philosophy of action, see Bill Pollard, 'Explaining Actions with Habits', *American Philosophical Quarterly* 43 (2006): 57–68, and 'Actions, Habits and Constitution', *Ratio* 19 (2006): 229–48.

17 John Locke, *An Essay concerning Human Understanding*, ed. P. H. Nidditch (Oxford: Clarendon Press, 1975), p. 293 (II.xxii.10).

18 Thomas Hobbes, *Elements of Philosophy, the First Section: Concerning Body*, in *The English Works of Thomas Hobbes*, vol. 4, ed. William Molesworth (London: J. Bohn, 1839), p. 349 (III.xxii.20).

19 Locke, *An Essay concerning Human Understanding*, p. 293 (II.xxii.10).

20 *Encyclopædia Britannica* (Edinburgh: 1771), vol. 2, p. 768.

21 Thomas Reid, *Essays on the Active Powers of Man* (Edinburgh, 1788), p. 117 (III.i.3).

22 Ibid., pp. 118–19.

23 The vibrant contemporary debate on the metaphysics of dispositions and powers lies beyond the scope of this essay. See in particular Stephen Mumford, *Dispositions* (Oxford: Oxford University Press, 2003); Stephen Mumford and Rani Lill Anjum, *Getting Causes from Powers* (Oxford: Oxford University Press, 2011); Anna Marmodoro (ed.), *The Metaphysics of Powers: Their Grounding and Their Manifestations* (London: Routledge, 2013).

24 See David Hume, *A Treatise of Human Nature*, ed. L. A. Selby-Bigge (Oxford: Clarendon Press, 1978), p. 167.

25 Søren Kierkegaard, *Repetition*, trans. Howard V. Hong and Edna H. Hong (Princeton: Princeton University Press, 1983), pp. 131; 186.

26 Ibid., p. 133.

27 For an extended discussion of this idea, see Catherine Pickstock, *Repetition and Identity* (Oxford: Oxford University Press, 2013), esp. ch. 3.

28 Claude Perrault, 'Du toucher', in *Oeuvres diverses de physique et de mécanique de Mrs. C. & P. Perrault* (Leyden, 1721), vol. 11, p. 547.

29 *Hegel's Philosophy of Mind*, p. 140 (§410).

30 Marcus Tullius Cicero, *De natura deorum*, trans. Horace C. R. McGregor (London: Penguin, 1972), p. 185.

31 *Hegel's Philosophy of Mind*, p. 141 (§410).

32 The concept of 'second nature' has received attention in recent years by philosophers interested in John McDowell's remarks on second nature and *Bildung*; see *Mind and World* (Cambridge, MA: Harvard University Press, 1996), pp. 84–88. On the relationship between the concepts of second nature offered by Hegel and McDowell, see Richard J. Bernstein, 'McDowell's Domesticated Hegelianism', in Nicholas Smith (ed.), *Reading McDowell: On Mind and World* (London: Routledge, 2002), pp. 9–24.

33 Félix Ravaisson, *Of Habit*, trans. Clare Carlisle and Mark Sinclair (London: Continuum, 2008), pp. 25, 31.

34 Aristotle, *Eudemian Ethics*, trans., ed. Brad Inwood and Raphael Woolf (Cambridge: Cambridge University Press, 2013), p. 19 (1120a–b); see also Henri Bergson, *Cours II: Leçons de psychologie, Leçons de morale, psychologie et métaphysique*, ed. H. Hude (Paris: Presses universitaire de France, 1992), p. 268.

35 See Plato, *Theaetetus* 197b–199c; A.-J. Festugière, *Contemplation et vie contemplative selon Platon* (Paris: Vrin, 1975), p. 292.

36 Aristotle, *Categories* 8b28–29. On Aristotle's concept of hexis, see Pierre Rodrigo, 'The Dynamic of *Hexis* in Aristotle's Philosophy', trans. Clare Carlisle, *Journal of the British Society for Phenomenology* 42, no. 1 (2011): 6–17.

37 Aristotle, *Nicomachean Ethics*, trans., ed. Roger Crisp (Cambridge: Cambridge University Press, 2000), p. 12 (1098a).

38 Gilles Deleuze, *Difference and Repetition*, trans. Paul Patton (London: Athlone, 1995), p. 95.

39 See Cathérine Malabou, *What Should We Do with Our Brain?*, trans. Sebastian Rand (New York: Fordham University Press, 2008), p. 13; Clare Carlisle, 'The Question of Habit in Theology and Philosophy: From *Hexis* to Plasticity', *Body & Society* 19, nos. 2 and 3 (2013): 30–57.

40 William James, *Psychology: Briefer Course* (Cambridge, MA: Harvard University Press, 1984), p. 126.

41 See D. H. Hebb, *The Organization of Behaviour: A Neuropsychological Theory* (London: Wiley & Sons, 1949); J. Konorski, *Conditioned Reflexes and Neuron Organization* (Cambridge: Cambridge University Press, 1948).

42 Ann M. Graybiel, 'Habits, Rituals and the Evaluative Brain', *Annual Review of Neuroscience* 31 (2008): 359–87, at pp. 361, 378.

43 See Malabou, *What Should We Do with Our Brain?*, pp. 33–38.

44 Robert Macfarlane, *The Old Ways* (London: Penguin, 2012), pp. 143, 228–29.

45 See John P. Wright, 'Ideas of Habit and Custom in Early Modern Philosophy' in *Journal of the British Society for Phenomenology* 42, no. 1 (2011): 18–32.

46 Nicolas Malebranche, *Search after Truth*, trans., ed. Thomas M. Lennon and Paul J. Olscamp (Cambridge: Cambridge University Press, 1997), p. 106; see also pp. 107–9.

47 Ibid., pp. 108, 134.

48 Locke, *Essay concerning Human Understanding*, p. 396 (II.xxxiii.6). This is in the chapter 'Of the Association of Ideas' added to the fourth edition of the *Essay* (1700).

49 Macfarlane, *The Old Ways*, p. 153.

50 Drawing on the ancient philosophical concepts of hexis and habitus, Edmund Husserl finds that as repeated actions become settled character traits, they become 'latent' or 'sedimented': 'No apprehension is merely momentary and ephemeral . . . This lived experience itself, and the objective moment constituted in it, may become "forgotten"; but for all this, it in no way disappears without a trace; it has merely become latent. With regard to what has been constituted in it, it is a *possession in the form of a habitus* ready at any time to be awakened anew by an active association'.

See Edmund Husserl, *Experience and Judgment: Investigations in a Genealogy of Logic*, trans. J. S. Churchill and K. Ameriks (Evanston: Northwestern University Press, 1973), p. 122; also Dermot Moran, 'Edmund Husserl's Phenomenology of Habituality and Habitus', *Journal of the British Society for Phenomenology* 42, no. 1 (2011): 53–77.

51 Ravaisson, *Of Habit*, p. 51.

52 Ibid.

53 Ibid., p. 29.

54 Joseph Butler, *The Analogy of Religion, Natural and Revealed, to the Constitution and Course of Nature* (Oxford: Oxford University Press, 1907), p. 102.

55 Ibid.

56 Hume, *A Treatise of Human Nature*, p. 424 (II.iii.5). On Hume's debt to Butler's discussion of habit, see John P. Wright, 'Butler and Hume on Habit and Moral Character', in M. A. Stewart and John P. Wright (eds), *Hume and Hume's Connexions* (University Park: Penn State University Press, 1995), pp. 105–18.

57 Hume, *A Treatise of Human Nature*, p. 423.

58 Xavier Bichat, *Physiological Researches on Life and Death*, trans. Tobias Watkins (Philadelphia: Smith & Maxwell, 1809), p. 34.

59 Ibid., pp. 36–37.

60 Ibid., p. 40.

61 Maine de Biran, *The Influence of Habit on the Faculty of Thinking*, p. 219.

62 Ravaisson, *Of Habit*, p. 37.

63 Ibid., p. 53.

64 See Clare Carlisle, 'Between Freedom and Necessity: Félix Ravaisson on Habit and the Moral Life', *Inquiry* 53, no. 2 (2010): 123–45.

65 Maine de Biran, *The Influence of Habit on the Faculty of Thinking*, pp. 49; 100–1.

Two

GOD OR DOG?

In Plato's *Republic* Socrates suggests that a philosopher is like a dog. Philosophers are distinguished by their 'love of wisdom', and this characteristic, he tells his pupil Glaucon, 'is something that you will discover in dogs'.[1] When Glaucon seems puzzled by this claim, Socrates points out that knowledge is a dog's sole evaluative principle. Dogs like what they know, being most attached to their master and their home, and are averse to strangers. A dog will 'distinguish a friendly from a hostile aspect by nothing save his apprehension of the one and his failure to recognise the other,' explains Socrates.

If Socrates' analogy surprises or amuses us, this is because it plays on the difference between two kinds of knowledge. The dog possesses knowledge by acquaintance, which has nothing to do with abstraction, calculation, or theorizing. Indeed, it is entirely compatible with naivety and even stupidity, and can be expressed by wagging one's tail, licking one's friends, and jumping up and down. The philosopher's knowledge, on the other hand, belongs to a refined and sophisticated intellect: it understands logic, geometry, and music; it strives to contemplate the highest realities; it reflects on the nature of justice, beauty, and goodness. According to Plato, it is almost divine.

Habit, born of familiarity and association, is more dog-like than god-like. The force of habit suggests a natural affinity with the known, and an aversion to the unknown. It often happens that in a new environment people quickly settle into a certain position. At the beginning of a conference, for example, you find a seat, either accidentally or by design, and then return to it (doggedly) at each new session, as if reassured by its familiarity. You may feel a stab of indignation to find someone in your place – that is, in an uncomfortable chair just like the others in the room. Or you return to the same table in a café, relieved to find it unoccupied. At the start of term, a class of students sit around a table, and without any compulsion or plan will often arrange themselves in the same way for the rest of the term. Like a loyal dog, habit loves what it knows, regardless of its inherent value.

If habit is also a form of knowledge in a more positive and instrumental sense, it is still opposed to the reflective kind of intelligence cultivated by philosophers. We may know the way to the local shop without being able to quantify its distance from home, or say whether its direction is north or south. We may know how to ride a bicycle without any idea how the gear and brake mechanisms work. We may recognize another person by his way of holding himself, without any understanding of anatomy. Sometimes theoretical knowledge can be drawn from habit, but it follows clumsily behind habit's assured proficiency. For example, a driver can, if she concentrates hard, tell her passenger how to send a text message on her mobile phone; or a teacher might explain to her students how to add a footnote to a document with a word-processor. Such explanations involve articulating inarticulate bodily movements, translating our habitual knowledge into a different kind of understanding.

Maine de Biran expresses a common philosophical view when he complains that habitual belief – 'blind faith! obstinate faith!' – is more influential than reason and evidence, 'to the shame of the human spirit.'[2] But since the early twentieth century both phenomenologists and pragmatists have attempted to invert the traditional preference for theoretical, reflective knowledge over practical, habitual knowledge. According to the phenomenologists, such a preference is a prejudice and a distortion that runs through our philosophical tradition. In *Being and Time* (1927) Martin Heidegger argues that a pre-reflective, practical kind of understanding underlies theoretical knowledge. He suggests that before we examine the world and its contents, attempting to find out what things are and how they work, we are already in a world that has meaning for us. This 'world' is not a physical space that can be measured, but a context in which certain projects and relationships matter to us, giving shape to our life. More simply, this world is our home. In describing our pre-theoretical 'Being-in-the-world', Heidegger uses the language of dwelling and habitation. The German word *Gewohnheit*, though similar in sense to the English 'habit' and the French *l'habitude*, has a different etymology: it comes from *wohnen*, meaning to live, in the sense of to dwell. The way we humans are 'in' this world is different from the way water is in a glass: we *inhabit* our world, experiencing it as our own – not in terms of a concept of property, but through an acquaintance that does not need to be conceptualized. According to Heidegger, traditional epistemology overlooks Being-in-the-world – precisely because this is too familiar, too *close to home* – so that philosophers such as Descartes take as their starting point a disembodied, homeless 'subject' who seeks to know alien objects in an alien world. The phenomenological method used in *Being and Time* involves describing familiar ways of being so that pre-reflective structures of existence, such as Being-in-the-world, can come into view.

Although there is little discussion of habit and embodiment in *Being and Time*, these concepts were seized on by other phenomenologists influenced by Heidegger's project. In *The Phenomenology of Perception* (1945) Maurice Merleau-Ponty points out that habit undermines the Cartesian division between an intelligent mind and a mechanical body, since in habit the body is animated by an unconscious intelligence. 'Habit', he writes, 'is knowledge in the hands'. While other French philosophers, including Ravaisson and Bergson, had regarded habit as following on from deliberate mental acts, Merleau-Ponty argues that habit need not depend on intellectual activity. 'Do we have to place at the origin of habit an act of the understanding which would organise its elements in order to withdraw itself later?', he asks, suggesting that 'it is the body which "catches" and "comprehends" movement: the acquisition of a habit is indeed the grasping of a significance, but it is the motor grasping of a motor significance.'[3]

Merleau-Ponty also emphasizes that knowledge acquired through habit is not simply mechanical conditioning or programming. Habit has a flexibility that enables it to adapt to different circumstances. For example, a skilled musician can easily pick up a new instrument, and an experienced driver can quickly adjust to a different car – even switching from left-hand to right-hand driving with little difficulty. In such cases, habit exhibits a responsive intelligence. Merleau-Ponty's contemporary Paul Ricoeur offers a similar interpretation of habit in his 1950 book *Freedom and Nature: The Voluntary and the Involuntary*. Ricoeur acknowledges that habitual knowledge can be machine-like, but he also highlights its adaptiveness and ingenuity. For Ricoeur, these different aspects of habit testify to its doubleness: it is 'at the same time a living spontaneity *and* an imitation of the automaton.' 'Our habits,' he concludes, 'are very ambiguous; it is not by chance that they lend themselves to two opposing systems of interpretation, in terms of life which learns and life which automatizes.'[4]

It is easy to see why these philosophers appeal to habitual knowledge in their critique of Cartesian dualism. Even if it is simplistic to argue that the 'knowledge in the hands' of a pianist or bus driver originates in bodily movements, without prior reflection, the idea that habits involve both the mind and the body also challenges the view that the mental and the physical are separate substances. However, even the phenomenologists recognize two distinct kinds of knowing: practical, implicit knowledge based on habit and familiarity, and reflective, explicit knowledge reached through rational thinking. Merleau-Ponty himself discusses what happens when these two forms of knowledge come into conflict: in the case of an amputee who has a 'phantom limb', the habit-body retains an awareness of the limb that is missing from the actual body. For Merleau-Ponty, this example shows that the body is not simply a physical phenomenon. But a more Cartesian interpretation is also plausible: the amputee has been led astray by his habit-body; he is quite simply *mistaken* about the existence of his arm or leg, and it is right that reason corrects this error. Habit will be his downfall if he tries to use his phantom limb to walk or to steady himself.

SPINOZA: HABITUAL THINKING

It is not only mind–body dualists who call into question the legitimacy of habitual knowledge. Spinoza, who offers a radical critique of Descartes' metaphysics in arguing that the mind and the body are aspects of a single substance, is also critical of habit. In Part 2 of his *Ethics* (1677) Spinoza discusses the nature of the human mind, its ways of being affected by external things, and its powers of understanding and interpretation. Here he distinguishes three kinds of knowledge: first, knowledge that comes through the imagination; second, knowledge that comes through reason; and, third, an intuitive knowledge which comprehends immediately the nature of things and their causal connections with one another.[5] The second and third kinds of knowledge both produce truthful or 'adequate' ideas – but imagination, which is regulated by habit, is an inadequate form of thought. Like Maine de Biran, Spinoza thinks that we fall into error when 'the order established by the habits of the imagination is confused with the nature of things.'[6] He identifies many 'prejudices' which persist because 'men judge things according to the disposition of their brain, and imagine, rather than understand them', and argues that 'all the notions by which ordinary people are accustomed to explain Nature are only modes of imagining, and do not indicate the nature of anything, only the constitution of the imagination.'[7]

According to Spinoza, the mind imagines when it perceives and interprets the images of bodies. He offers a physical account of the production of images, which rests on a basic principle of his philosophy: bodies affect, and are affected by, other bodies. When a body comes 'frequently' into contact with an external body, 'it changes its surface and, as it were, impresses on it certain traces [*vestigia*].'[8] In other words, bodies are characterized by plasticity: they are receptive to changes and can be modified by them, but they can also hold their form, so that 'traces' remain in bodies to mark the way in which they have been affected. Images are the mental correlate of these bodily traces, and imagining involves joining together a series of images in the mind, according to a certain manner of interpretation. And habit is integral to this process of drawing meaning from physical interactions: it is 'association', or habit, that links one image to another. 'For example,' explains Spinoza, 'from the thought of the word *pomum* a Roman will immediately pass to the thought of the fruit, which has no similarity to that articulate sound and nothing in common with it except that the body of the same man has often been affected by these two, that is, that the man often heard the word *pomum* while he saw the fruit.' There is no intrinsic connection between the image of the word and the image of the apple. Nevertheless, the connection that is supplied by frequent association is 'immediate': it does not require reflection or calculation. 'And in this way,' Spinoza continues, 'each of us will pass from one thought to another, as each one's association [*consuetudo*] has ordered the images of things in the body.'[9]

He illustrates this important point by comparing the way two people will interpret the same sign: 'A soldier, having seen traces of a horse in the sand, will immediately pass from the thought of a horse to the thought of a horseman, and from that to the thought of war, and so on. But a farmer will pass from the thought of a horse to the thought of a plough, and then to that of a field, and so on.' The order of the imagination is the order of habit. And this order is historical, since it reflects an individual's previous experience: 'so each one, according as he has been accustomed to join and connect the images of things in this or that way, will pass from one thought to another.' Spinoza develops this idea by describing how habitual associations are projected into the future, forming expectations based on what has happened in the past. He gives the example of a child who yesterday saw Peter in the morning, Paul at noon, and Simon in the evening. When the little boy sees Peter again the following morning, he anticipates the same sequence of events that he observed the previous day: 'as soon as he sees the morning light, he will immediately imagine the sun taking the same course through the sky, or he will imagine the whole day, and Peter together with the morning, Paul with noon, and Simon with the evening. That is, he will imagine the existence of Paul and of Simon with a relation to future time.' Through habit, then, imagination stretches from what is past to what lies ahead. Experience, because it is the source of habit, can produce a sense of the future.

Towards the end of Part 2 of the *Ethics*, Spinoza extends his analysis of habitual thinking in considering general concepts, or 'common notions'. Here, the image in question is not a mark in the sand, but the concept of humanity. Interpretations of this image will vary, he explains, according to our bodily dispositions:

> For example, those who have more often regarded men's stature with wonder will understand by the word *man* an animal of erect stature. But those who have been accustomed to consider something else, will form another common image of men – for example, that man is an animal capable of laughter, or a featherless biped, or a rational animal. And similarly concerning the others – each will form universal images of things according to the disposition of his body.[10]

Again, Spinoza is suggesting that the way we interpret images reveals more about our past experience than about the nature of external things. The chain of images in our mind reflects our particular habit, and no one will share exactly the same sequence or 'concatenation' of images with another person. Habit, then, is a subjective principle, and there is nothing to guarantee its application to objective reality. Indeed, Spinoza argues that the mind has 'only a confused knowledge, of itself, of its own body, and of external bodies, so long as it is determined externally, from fortuitous encounters with things.'[11] This knowledge by association is 'without order for the intellect', since it is drawn 'from random experience.'[12]

Spinoza thinks that genuine knowledge is gained by making the transition from imagination to reason – from the first to the second kind of knowledge. This involves a reordering of thought. Instead of following the order of habit, our thinking should follow the order of nature, or reality. According to Spinoza, this order is both logical and causal, for ideas are connected logically and things are connected causally. Since 'the order and connection of ideas is the same as the order and connection of things', truly knowing something means understanding its causes – grasping how it fits into the whole of nature, to which it belongs and on which it depends. Spinoza contrasts imagination, which follows 'the order and connection of the affections of the human body', with 'the connection of ideas which happens according to the order of the intellect, by which the mind perceives things through their first causes, and which is the same in all men.'[13]

Although the imagination seems to be more subjective than reason, it is in becoming rational that a person learns to think for herself. According to Spinoza, the transition from habit to reason is a shift from passivity to activity. In developing adequate knowledge, we become less subject to the vicissitudes of fortune, which bring us into contact with this or that external influence, and generate this or that sequence of associations. Through rational thought we come to understand the nature of things, and how they affect one another, and this empowers us to order our own experience in a way that harmonizes with reality and promotes our happiness. So, whereas habitual thinking is based on experience, and subject to its contingency, rational thinking provides the basis for a wiser, more philosophical way of life.

When we attend to our own mental activity, Spinoza's critique of habitual thinking starts to appear even more radical than his critique of Descartes' metaphysics. Most of us will find a constant stream of thoughts passing through our minds, jumping from one train of associations to another. When we see that our thinking is far more often passive than active, we realize that we are seldom the authors of our thoughts. It is difficult to disrupt the flow of images or ideas for longer than a few seconds, such is the force of habit. And it takes real effort to sustain a rational train of thought without distraction, even for a couple of minutes. In criticizing habitual, imaginative thinking, Spinoza is not talking about an aberration, nor something that is confined to a certain group of people (the uneducated, the stupid, or the insane), but calling into question virtually all our ordinary mental activity. And he emphasizes that the transition from habitual to rational thought is extremely difficult, and rarely achieved.

HUME: THE GREAT GUIDE OF LIFE

About sixty years after the publication of the *Ethics*, Hume outlined an account of habitual thinking which echoes Spinoza's in many respects. Where Spinoza writes of a sequence of images, Hume describes an association of ideas in the imagination – ideas which have their source in sense impressions. Hume's immediate influence here is not Spinoza, but Locke, who added a chapter on the association of ideas to the fourth edition of his *Essay concerning Human Understanding* (1700).[14] Locke criticizes the association of ideas that comes from 'Chance or Custom', as opposed to the more 'natural' connection of ideas that can be found through rational thinking. According to Locke, the habitual association of ideas, often brought about by indoctrination at an early age, is responsible for irrational religious or political beliefs, and even leads to a 'sort of Madness'.

While both Locke and Spinoza contrast habitual, imaginative thinking with reason, which alone yields sound judgements, Hume regards the association of ideas as the most important principle of the human mind. He argues that much of the thinking that other philosophers ascribe to reason is rooted in habit – that, for example, the 'education' or 'indoctrination' so disdained by Locke is 'built almost on the same foundation of custom and repetition as our reasonings from cause and effect.'[15] In the first book of his *Treatise of Human Nature* (1739), Hume suggests that the association of ideas, in which habit plays a crucial role, is the basis of our most fundamental judgements: those concerning causal connections, personal identity, and an external world existing independently of our perceptions. The associations of ideas in the imagination are, he claims, 'the only ties of our thoughts', 'the cement of the universe', and therefore 'all the operations of the mind must, in a great measure, depend on them.'[16] This view of habit is highly original: 'Hume's remarkable discovery is that nature itself teaches us through the same principle of association which is also the source of our prejudice and pathological thinking.'[17]

Hume identifies three principles of association: '*Resemblance*; a picture naturally makes us think of the man it was drawn for. *Contiguity*; when *St. Denis* is mentioned, the idea of *Paris* naturally occurs. *Causation*; when we think of the son, we are apt to carry our attention to the father.'[18] The second and third of these, at least, are due to habit. Although in the *Treatise* Hume goes so far as to claim that 'all belief and reasoning' can be attributed to 'custom', he does not offer a detailed account of custom, or habit, itself. He simply points out that 'we call every thing CUSTOM, which proceeds from a past repetition, without any new reasoning or conclusion', before stating that 'when we are accustom'd to see two impressions conjoin'd together, the appearance or idea of the one immediately carries us to the idea of the other.'[19] As we have seen, Spinoza had already drawn attention to the immediacy of habitual connections, and Hume emphasizes that 'custom operates before we have time for reflexion', that 'we interpose not a moment's delay' in passing from one object to another which customarily follows it.[20] This automatic, unreflective character of habit makes it quasi-natural, since it resembles instinct. But while Spinoza thinks that reflection ought to 'interpose' itself to disrupt habit and correct its errors, Hume seems happy to let habitual thinking flow along in its easy manner. He certainly recognizes habit's power to maintain ideas that reason or reflection would recognize as erroneous, for he offers several examples of this:

> A person, that has lost a leg or an arm by amputation, endeavours for a long time afterwards to serve himself with them. After the death of any one, 'tis a common remark of the whole family, but especially of the servants, that they can scarce believe him to be dead, but still

imagine him to be in his chamber or in any other place, where they were accustom'd to find him . . . As liars, by the frequent repetition of their lies, come at last to remember them; so the judgment, or rather the imagination, by the like means, may have ideas so strongly imprinted on it, and conceive them in so full a light, that they may operate upon the mind in the same manner with those, which the senses, memory or reason present to us.[21]

Hume does not here urge us to discard or overcome our habitual ways of thinking. Instead, he wants to challenge those 'philosophers' who criticize habit in the name of a superior, more rational form of thought.

Hume also echoes Spinoza in pointing out that habit makes us anticipate that the future will follow the same course as the past. He remarks on the general principle that 'a constant perseverance in any course of life produces a strong inclination and tendency to continue for the future', but in applying this to inductive reasoning – which makes judgements based on previous experience – Hume arrives at a surprising conclusion: that such inferences are not rational. All induction has to presume that the future will resemble the past; only with this presumption can we predict what will happen on the basis of what we have previously observed. For example, we might feel sure that the sun will set at a certain time tomorrow evening. But our conviction rests on our belief that things will continue to follow the same patterns as they have done before. And our only basis for this belief is the fact that in the past such patterns have been followed with strict regularity. Again, we are relying on previous experience and simply assuming that it provides a reliable guide to the future. When we make explicit the processes of reasoning at work in such a quotidian judgement, it becomes clear that we are 'going in a circle, and taking that for granted, which is the very point in question.'[22]

So in fact, argues Hume, our inductive inferences are based, not on reason, but on habit: 'the supposition, *that the future resembles the past*, is not founded on arguments of any kind, but is deriv'd entirely from habit, by which we are determin'd to expect for the future the same train of objects, to which we have been accustom'd.'[23] Of course, it is not only commonplace, informal predictions that rest upon this expectation, but any scientific theory that draws on experimental observations. This means that habit plays a crucial role in making nature intelligible, and in his *Enquiries concerning Human Understanding* Hume concludes that 'it is that principle alone which renders our experience useful to us, and makes us expect, for the future, a similar train of events with those that have appeared in the past. Without the influence of custom, we should be entirely ignorant of every matter of fact beyond what is immediately present to the memory and senses.'[24] So, while Hume's empiricist principle that experience is the only source of our ideas and so-called 'knowledge' leads him to recognize the importance of habit, it is habit itself that, so to speak, breaks through this empiricism. Habit produces a belief about the relationship between the past and the future − a belief that cannot be legitimated by our experience.

Hume's view of habit has similarly radical implications for causal reasoning. Since the judgement that one thing or event causes another seems to imply that there is a necessary connection between them, other philosophers had regarded this as a relation to be apprehended by reason. But for Hume our belief in necessary connections arises from the habitual association of ideas:

> The idea of cause and effect is deriv'd from experience, which presenting us with certain objects constantly conjoin'd with each other, produces such a habit of surveying them in that relation, that we cannot without a sensible violence survey them in any other . . . After a frequent repetition, I find, that upon the appearance of one [object], the mind is *determin'd* by custom to consider its usual attendant . . . 'Tis this impression, then, or *determination*, which affords me the idea of necessity.[25]

Hume uses the phrase 'sensible violence' to suggest that the force of habit – the link between two ideas in the imagination – is something that we *feel*, and that this link is so strong, and appears so natural, that breaking it seems violent and destructive. Here again we encounter the idea that habit is a second nature: a force that has the same immediacy as instinct, and the same apparent necessity.

Whereas Spinoza places habit on the wrong side of a divide between irrational prejudice and rational knowledge, Hume uses the concept of habit to undermine this distinction. While Spinoza's rationalism leads him to contrast the inadequacy of habitual knowledge, drawn from experience, with the genuine understanding attained by reason, Hume insists that experience is the only source of knowledge. Even if there were a distinct rational order that our thinking ought to follow, Hume believes that we have no access to this order, for all our ideas come from the 'impressions' received by our senses. So Hume's empiricism commits him to the view that habit is the only order available to us. One consequence of this is that the supposedly superior kind of thinking practised by philosophers and scientists is no more rational, and no less prejudiced, than the superstitious beliefs of those whom philosophers of the period tended to call 'the vulgar'. If both kinds of thinking rely on the association of ideas, they are equally guided by habit. In Hume's philosophy, 'prejudice' can no longer be a derogatory term: all judgement rests on pre-judgment or presumption, and it is habit that provides the 'before' from which we infer an 'after'. This inference might not be rational, but it is simply the way we naturally think about the world. So while Spinoza believes that habit leads us into error, Hume regards it as 'the great guide of human life' since, as we have seen, it makes our experience 'useful to us'. And this is a pragmatic judgment: for Hume, the criterion of habit's value is its usefulness, rather than its truth – for we can discover no independent standard of truth that our thinking could be assessed against.

RATIONAL HABITUATION

Although Spinoza denies that habitual thinking can produce knowledge of the nature and causes of things, he does not think that reason should simply replace habit. In fact, in spite of his rationalism, he gives habit a vital role in reordering our thinking 'according to the intellect'. Having presented a lengthy discussion of the emotions, or 'affects', in Part 4 of the Ethics, Spinoza turns in Part 5 to consider how these affects can be brought into harmony with a rational understanding of both ourselves and others. 'So long as we are not torn by affects contrary to our nature, we have the power of ordering and connecting the affections of the body according to the order of the intellect,' he writes.[26] Spinoza argues that once we completely understand our emotions we will cease to be subject to them – but he acknowledges that this kind of self-knowledge is difficult to achieve. 'So long as we do not have perfect knowledge of our affects,' he advises, 'the best thing we can do is to conceive a correct principle of living, or sure maxims of life, to commit them to memory, and to apply them constantly to the particular cases frequently encountered in life.'[27]

Here we find an instance of habit acting as both problem and solution – as a *pharmakon*. Having been identified as a poison, habit reappears as the cure. Like the Stoics, Spinoza advocates imaginative practices that will retrain the mind to follow a certain order of associations. By way of an example, he suggests that the ethical maxim 'that hate is to be conquered by love, by not repaying it with hate in return' should be joined to the image of wrongdoing by 'frequently' meditating on 'the common wrongs of men, and how they might be warded off best by nobility'. In this way, the maxim 'will always be ready for us when a wrong is done to us.'[28] Similarly, he says that the emotion of fear can be conquered if we 'recount and frequently imagine the common dangers of life, and how they can be best avoided and overcome by presence of mind and strength of character.' Here, as he explains how these imaginative practices change the mind's patterns of thinking, Spinoza refers the reader back to his analysis of habituation in Part 2 of the *Ethics*. And he reminds us that 'as an image is related to more things, the more frequent it is, or the more often it flourishes, and the more it engages the mind.' On the basis of this principle, Spinoza proposes the most important practice of all: relating all the body's affections, and all images of things, to the idea of God. This is not simply a moral or religious exercise, but a philosophical one: its goal is true understanding, not just virtuous or pious behaviour. Spinoza's God is not a transcendent Creator, but a non-anthropomorphic power that is the 'immanent cause' of all things, the Being of all beings. So to associate things with this idea of God is to link them to the idea of their cause – and for Spinoza, this is precisely what it means to have genuine knowledge.

The style of the *Ethics* reflects this account of mental training. The text is written according to a geometrical method, beginning with definitions and axioms and then presenting a sequence of interlinked propositions which, Spinoza claims, follow necessarily from what precedes them. Beginning with basic metaphysical terminology – cause, substance, mode, attribute, and so on – Spinoza advances a conception of God as a single eternal substance possessing infinite attributes, and goes on to show how 'from the necessity of the divine nature there must follow infinitely many things in infinitely many modes'.[29] The *Ethics* does not just offer a certain account of reality. It seems to be designed to function as a kind of training manual, which gets its readers' minds accustomed to following the logical and ontological order of reality – beginning with the cause of all things – instead of the random order of their own experience. The right way of reading the text, then, would be to return to it often and repeatedly. And Spinoza encourages this, by frequently referring his readers back to earlier definitions and propositions.

On the one hand, then, Spinoza advocates a reordering of thought from the fortuitous sequence of experience, which generates habit, to the logical and causal order that constitutes knowledge. But on the other hand, he invokes the mechanism of habit – that is, the repeated association of ideas – to explain how our thinking can be reordered in accordance with rational principles. Reason does not banish habit altogether; instead, it utilizes habit's power to form the mind. Because reason understands habit – because it grasps the causal processes at work in habit acquisition – it can turn these processes to its own ends. Left to itself, habit leads people away from the truth, but in the hands of the philosopher it becomes an instrument for cultivating wisdom.

Spinoza's *Ethics* provides a particularly good illustration of how habit acts as a *pharmakon* which, though it may lead us astray, can also be used for correction and improvement. But this idea can be found elsewhere. In the *Meditations* (1641), for example, Descartes proposes a method of searching for certain knowledge that involves disrupting customary beliefs and habitual ways of thinking, but he also stresses the importance of cultivating a habit of attention to our own judgements. He discovers that he falls into error when his will exceeds his intellect – that is, when he wants to form judgements about things that he doesn't properly understand. Since reason alone cannot overcome the fallibility of his knowledge, habit has to come to the rescue:

> Even if I have no power to avoid error [by having] a clear perception of everything I have to deliberate on, I can avoid error [simply by] remembering to withhold judgment on any occasion when the truth of the matter is not clear. Admittedly, I am aware of a certain weakness in me, in that I am unable to keep my attention fixed on one and the same item of knowledge at all times; but by attentive and repeated meditation I am nevertheless able to make myself remember it as often as the need arises, and thus get into the habit of avoiding error.[30]

Descartes turns this personal experience into a practical principle in a letter, dated September 1645, to Princess Elisabeth of Bohemia. Elisabeth, who was troubled by various health problems and administrative responsibilities, sought the philosopher's advice about how to live more in accordance with reason. Descartes acknowledges that 'it is not so much the theory but the practice which is difficult in this matter,'[31] and he reflects on the difference between 'theoretical knowledge' and 'practical knowledge':

> Besides knowledge of the truth, habituation is also required for being always disposed to judge well. For since we cannot always be attentive to the same thing – even though we have been convinced of some truth by reason of some clear and evident perceptions – we will be able to be turned, afterward, to believing false appearances, if we do not, after long and frequent meditation, imprint it sufficiently in our mind so that it turns into habit. In this sense, the Schools are right to say that the virtues are habits, for one rarely makes a mistake because one doesn't have theoretical knowledge of what to do, but only because one doesn't have practical knowledge, that is to say, because one doesn't have a firm habit of believing it.[32]

Descartes elegantly concludes this letter by adding, 'And so, as while I here examine these truths, I also augment my habit of believing them, I am particularly obligated to your Highness for permitting me this exchange.' Like Spinoza, Descartes sets the standard for knowledge very high, but then acknowledges the difficulty of attaining it – and recommends a practice that will gradually train an imperfect mind to avoid error.

Of course, techniques that utilize the power of habit to reform the mind are not confined to a philosophical context. Many religious practices, based on the principle of frequent repetition, are designed to replace bad habits of thinking with good ones – to not only curb but reverse a tendency to turn towards temptations and away from God. Christian training manuals such as *The Rule of St Benedict* and Ignatius Loyola's *Spiritual Exercises* formalize this process and make it explicit. And more recently, in a therapeutic context, a similar method is used in techniques like cognitive behavioural therapy, which treats depression and anxiety by providing a structured programme of habit replacement. People undergoing cognitive behavioural therapy bring their unnoticed mental habits into view by recording thoughts and feelings several times each day, and then train themselves to replace negative patterns of thinking with more positive ones. In other words, the method reorders what philosophers such as Locke and Hume called 'the association of ideas'.

The similarity between ancient religious practices and contemporary therapeutic techniques has often been remarked upon. But underlying the common features of these approaches to mental reform – frequent and regular practice, and attentiveness to the association of ideas – is a significant difference. Whereas religious practices aim to reorder habit according to a conception of reality, so that the practitioner is led away from error and into truth, modern therapeutic practices operate according to a more pragmatic model. This difference is a philosophical one: indeed, it echoes the contrast between Spinoza's rationalism and Hume's pragmatic empiricism. In common with Spinoza, Catholic teachers like Benedict and Ignatius ground their programmes of reform on ideals of truth and goodness that can, at least in principle, be known to us – whether by reason or by an experience of divine revelation. The techniques devised by modern psychiatry are regulated, in a more Humean spirit, by criteria of well-being rather than truth, for they aim to accomplish a transition from positive to negative states of mind, from mental illness to mental health.

NATURE'S HABITS

Comparing the views of Hume and Spinoza yields interesting insights into the relationship between habit and knowledge. From Hume's empiricist perspective, it is habit that makes experience intelligible; according to Spinoza's rationalism, habit makes reason effective. Habit supplements and also points beyond both empiricism and rationalism, signalling the limits of these epistemological positions. While he invokes habit to explain most of our beliefs, Hume denies that we can gain knowledge of habit itself. If we know only what we observe from experience, then we cannot know habit as a cause or principle of action, for all we see of habit is frequent and regular repetition. And if we do not know what habit is or how it works then its explanatory power must be limited.

The main problem with Spinoza's view is that he, like Hume, regards habit only as a subjective or psychological principle.[33] According to both philosophers, habit is a process that happens in the imagination and is then projected 'outside' the mind, onto the world. As Hume famously puts it, 'the mind has a great propensity to spread itself over external objects.'[34] Although Spinoza does think that rational and intuitive thinking can penetrate into the nature of things and understand their causes, he sees this kind of thinking as quite different from the work of the imagination. He seems to regard habit merely as a kind of culture – something that is acquired in a process akin to indoctrination – and not as an aspect or a principle of nature. And this means that he treats habit as simply a way of thinking, and not also a way of being; as something that inhibits our understanding, rather than as something that needs to be understood if we are to understand nature as a whole. As Gilles Deleuze writes in his 1953 book on Hume, *Empiricism and Subjectivity*, 'the paradox of habit [is] that it is formed by degrees and also that it is a principle of human nature.'[35] In other words, habits themselves are acquired, but the principle of habit acquisition is innate in all of us. To call this a 'paradox' is perhaps questionable, since there is a difference between habit (singular) considered as a principle, and particular habits (plural) that are acquired. Nevertheless, Deleuze points here to a double aspect of habit, which Spinoza does not seem to have grasped: human habit is natural as well as cultural, innate as well as acquired.

This so-called 'paradox of habit' is sharpened by the suggestion that habit belongs not just to human nature, but to the natures of other animals, plants, and even crystals. Surely the 'pathways' forged through habit are not simply in our own minds, but in the minds and bodies of other beings, and also in the landscape, revealing patterns of life, movement and growth. Habits are created through experience, acquired gradually through our encounters and interactions, and yet they already belong to the things that form the content of this experience.

The idea that habit is not simply a subjective, psychological principle but an objective principle of nature has been developed through the modern period. It finds an early expression in the seventeenth century: Leibniz uses the concept of habit to defend belief in miracles against the protest (voiced by Spinoza, among others) that miraculous events transgress and disrupt divinely ordained laws of nature. In his *Discourse on Metaphysics*, written in the 1680s, Leibniz argues that the 'natural' order of things 'is only a habit of God' (*n'est qu'une coustoume de Dieu*) — a habit that God can choose to break whenever there is a 'stronger reason' to do so.[36] Elsewhere, Leibniz refers to the 'habits of the world' (*consuetudine mundi*) to make a similar point.[37]

A more naturalistic version of this idea of cosmic habit begins to emerge in the essays *de l'habitude* by Maine de Biran and Ravaisson. Both these philosophers suggest that a certain kind of introspection allows them to move beyond empiricism — a stance which, as Hume and Reid found, yields no positive insight into the operations of habit.[38] Until we turn our attention upon ourselves, admits Ravaisson, 'nature is a spectacle for us that we can only see from the outside. We see only the exteriority of the actuality of things; we do not see their dispositions or powers.' But unlike the empiricists, he thinks that we do have access to the principles underlying our own activity: 'In consciousness, by contrast, the same being at once acts and sees the act; or better, the act and the apprehension of the act are fused together . . . It is only in consciousness that we can aspire not just to establish [habit's] apparent law but to learn its *how* and its *why*, to illuminate its generation, and finally to understand its cause.'[39] While Ravaisson regards habit as a 'way of being' of everything that has a nature — that is, of all things that can move themselves and be affected by other things — he does not simply assume that our knowledge of human habit can be transferred to nature as a whole. However, he argues that the 'powerful' analogy between nature and second nature permits us to apply what we learn from observing habit within our own minds and bodies to the operations of nature. Although he maintains the distinction between habit and instinct, and between habitual regularity and natural law, Ravaisson treats 'second nature' as a mirror of nature itself. By looking into the mirror of habit, he suggests, we can peer into the inwardness of things that are otherwise inaccessible to empirical study. The great chain of being 'is like a spiral whose principle lies in the depths of nature, and yet which ultimately flourishes in consciousness' – and, continues Ravaisson, 'Habit comes back down this spiral, teaching us of its origins and genesis.'[40]

Bergson draws attention to the philosophical implications of this idea in his discourse on Ravaisson, which he delivered when he succeeded the author of *De l'habitude* to the Académie des Sciences morales et politiques:

> Our inner experience shows us in habit an activity which has passed, by imperceptible degrees, from consciousness to unconsciousness and from will to automatism. Should we not then imagine nature, in this form, as an obscured consciousness and a dormant will? Habit thus gives us a living demonstration of this truth, that mechanism is not sufficient to itself: it is, so to speak, only the fossilised residue of a spiritual activity.[41]

Ravaisson is a typically post-Kantian thinker in his critique of mechanistic theories of nature and in his effort to move beyond the limitations of both rationalism and empiricism. And, indeed, his essay *De l'habitude* combines features of the accounts of habit provided by Spinoza and Hume. Like Hume, he has a positive conception of habit and is prepared to see it as a legitimate source of knowledge. Like Spinoza, he thinks that human beings can gain insight into objective reality – but, crucially, he recognizes that habit is part of this reality. This means that we do not have to overcome the influence of subjective habit in order to understand things as they are in themselves. Rather, knowledge harmonizes subjective and objective habit, in the belief that the associations of ideas within our own minds can at least mirror connections that underlie the patterns and regularities we perceive in the world.

Towards the end of the nineteenth century, several philosophers advanced a stronger version of the idea that habit is a principle of nature as a whole, in arguing that so-called laws of nature are long-standing, deeply entrenched habitual patterns. In 'A Guess at the Riddle' (1887–88), Charles Sanders Peirce states that 'three elements are active in the world: first, chance; second, law; and third, habit-taking . . . All things have a tendency to take habits. For atoms and their parts, molecules and groups of molecules, and in short every conceivable real object, there is a greater probability of acting as on a former like occasion than otherwise.'[42] Peirce's contemporary William James asserts, more robustly, that 'the laws of Nature are nothing but the immutable habits which the different elementary sorts of matter follow in their actions and reactions upon each other.'[43] A variation of this thesis is developed by Émile Boutroux, who in the early 1900s delivered the Gifford Lectures in Glasgow on 'Nature and Spirit'. Boutroux's reputation was built on his doctoral thesis, *La contingence des lois de la nature*, published in 1874 – a work that draws on Darwinian and Lamarckian theories of evolution. Boutroux argues here that 'animal instinct, life, physical and mechanical forces are, as it were, habits that have penetrated more and more deeply into the spontaneity of being. Hence these habits have become almost unconquerable. Seen from without, they appear as necessary laws.'[44]

In a similar vein, Samuel Butler's *Life and Habit* (1878) proposes that habit and memory account for the formation of plant and animal species. In speaking of 'inherited habit' – a concept that is employed by both Darwin and Lamarck – Butler undermines the customary distinction between habit and instinct.[45] 'Plants and animals only differ from one another because they remember different things,' writes Butler; 'plants and animals only grow up in the shapes they assume because this shape is their memory, their idea concerning their own past history . . . Life, then, is memory: we are all the same stuff to start with, but we remember different things.'[46] The 'memory' in question here is really habit, rather than recollection, since it is unconscious as well as involuntary. Butler identifies a spectrum of habits, from those which are peculiarly human, such as 'speech, the upright posture, the arts and sciences', to those which we have least control over and consciousness of, such as 'digestion and circulation, which belonged even to our invertebrate ancestry, and which are habits, geologically speaking, of extreme antiquity.'[47] However, he follows Lamarck in attributing the formation of habits to 'an intelligent sense of need', instead of invoking just 'use and disuse', as Darwin does in *On the Origin of Species*. Butler draws a bold conclusion from his observations on habit:

We must suppose the continuity of life and sameness between living beings, whether plants or animals, and their descendants, to be far closer than we have hitherto believed, so that the experience of one person is not enjoyed by his successor, so much as that the successor is *bonâ fide* but a part of the life of his progenitor, imbued with all his memories, profiting by all his experiences – which are, in fact, his own – and only unconscious of the extent of his own memories and experiences owing to their vastness and already infinite repetitions.[48]

The view that the difference between acquired habit and natural law or instinct is simply a matter of longevity remains on the margins of contemporary scientific discourse.[49] From a philosophical point of view, Butler and Boutroux and their pragmatist contemporaries seem to be offering rather speculative theories of nature. But in making their claims for the importance of habit throughout the natural world, they are perhaps emboldened by their acquaintance with habit in their own experience. Of course, if they were right to believe in the close 'continuity of life and sameness between living beings', as Butler puts it, then reflection on human habit would indeed yield insight into the unobservable principles of nature.

Deleuze brings together the psychological and biological (or subjective and objective) accounts of habit to develop an empiricist alternative to Kantian transcendental philosophy. While Kant posits an atemporal 'transcendental subject' that is the condition of the possibility of human experience, Deleuze argues that our actual experience is conditioned by a subjectivity formed in and through experience, 'defined by the movement through which it develops'.[50] Although this self-constitution happens in time, it involves a synthesis or ordering of time. In *Empiricism and Subjectivity* Deleuze suggests that 'habit is the constitutive root of the subject, and the subject, at its root, is the synthesis of time – the synthesis of the present and the past in the light of the future.'[51] In his 1989 preface to the English translation of this text, he adds that 'we are habits, nothing but habits – the habit of saying "I". Perhaps there is no more striking answer to the problem of the Self.'[52]

These ideas are developed at greater length in *Difference and Repetition*, where habit is explicated in terms of 'contemplation' and 'contraction'. Deleuze argues here that we acquire habits not through action, as (he says) psychologists assume, but through contemplation. This concept denotes a 'passive synthesis' that draws and holds together repeated elements, and thus comprises an ever-expanding past. Understood in this way, contemplation is essentially temporal: 'We are habits . . . We exist only in contemplating – that is to say, in contracting that from which we come.'[53] Passive synthesis 'constitutes our habit of living, our expectation that "it" will continue.'[54] Deleuze argues that contemplation or contraction brings order to flux by finding a kind of rhythm of differences. From bare movements, fluctuations, and transitions – for example, relaxing or contracting – there emerges a sequence, a pulse, 'successive tick-tocks' that are fused together in the process of contemplation. The elements that are repeated in this basic habit formation, then, are differences: the difference between relaxation and contraction, between degrees of intensity, between 'tick' and 'tock'.

In systematizing or regulating these differences, habit begins to generate the recognizable identity and unity which we call a self, and which is supposed to underlie the activities of perceiving, judging, understanding, choosing and so on. But although Deleuze talks about a 'contemplating mind' or a 'contemplating soul', he attributes this to the most elemental life forms: 'what organism is not made up of elements and cases of repetition, of contemplated and contracted water, nitrogen, carbon, chlorides and sulphates, thereby intertwining all the habits of which it is composed?'[55] Throughout nature, then, habit is the beginning of identity, and to say that something 'has a nature' is, for Deleuze, to recognize it as habitual. This reverses the more familiar idea – which, as we saw in Chapter 1, goes back to Aristotle – that only those entities which have a modifiable nature can acquire habits. We also saw in the previous chapter that both receptivity and resistance to change (or, in other words, to differences) are conditions of habit acquisition. Deleuze seems to prioritize receptivity with his concept of the contemplative soul, which is 'like a sensitive plate',[56] although perhaps the holding together accomplished in passive synthesis echoes an idea of hexis, and constitutes a nascent principle of resistance to change.

While Deleuze's ontology of habit is naturalistic, it is also poetic. 'There is a beatitude associated with passive synthesis,' he writes: 'By its existence alone, the lily of the field sings the glory of the heavens, the goddesses and the gods – in other words, the elements that it contemplates in contracting.'[57] Indeed, contraction and contemplation are apt metaphors for a philosopher who draws together and – somehow – synthesizes the diverse work of successive thinkers: Spinoza, Leibniz, Hume, Kant, Husserl, Bergson (and, via Bergson, Ravaisson). In contemplating these different philosophies, Deleuze produces a new habit of thinking, and thereby challenges our thinking about habit. If, as he argues, philosophy consists in the creation of concepts, this involves the creation of habits – for both concepts and habits of thinking come about by crystallizing patterns of associations, formations of 'new connections, new pathways, new synapses'.[58] This sounds exciting, and we might need to be reminded that our intellectual creativity may be for better or for worse – lest we fall into the habit of associating 'the new' too closely with the good.

1 Plato, *Republic*, trans. Tom Griffith, ed. G. R. F. Ferrari (Cambridge: Cambridge University Press, 2000), pp. 59–60 (375e–376b).

2 Maine de Biran, *The Influence of Habit on the Faculty of Thinking*, trans. Margaret Donaldson Boehm (Westport, CT: Greenwood Press, 1970), p. 195.

3 Maurice Merleau-Ponty, *The Phenomenology of Perception*, trans. Colin Smith (London: Routledge, 1962), p. 144. On habitual knowledge in Merleau-Ponty, see Emmanuel de Saint Aubert, ' "C'est le corps qui comprend": Le sens de l'habitude chez Merleau-Ponty', *Alter* 12 (2004): 105–28.

4 Paul Ricoeur, *Freedom and Nature: The Voluntary and the Involuntary*, trans. Erazim V. Kohák (Evanston, IL: Northwestern University Press, 1966), p. 297; *Fallible Man*, trans. Charles Kelby (Chicago: Henry Regnery, 1967), p. 88.

5 See Spinoza, *Ethics*, trans. Edwin Curley, E2P40, scholia.

6 Maine de Biran, *The Influence of Habit on the Faculty of Thinking*, p. 222.

7 Spinoza, *Ethics*, E1, Appendix.

8 Ibid., E2, postulate 5.

9 Ibid., E2P18, scholium.

10 Ibid., E2P40, scholium 1.

11 Ibid., E2P29, scholium.

12 Ibid., E2P40, scholium 2.

13 Ibid., E2P18, scholium.

14 Hume does not seem to have read Spinoza's works, but he was certainly acquainted with Spinoza's controversial religious and metaphysical views – he read about them in Pierre Bayle's *Historical and Critical Dictionary*, which contains a lengthy article on Spinoza.

15 David Hume, *A Treatise of Human Nature*, 2nd edn, ed. L. A. Selby-Bigge and P. H. Nidditch (Oxford: Clarendon Press, 1978), p. 117.

16 Ibid., p. 662 ('An Abstract of *A Treatise of Human Nature*').

17 John P. Wright, *Hume's 'A Treatise of Human Nature'* (Cambridge: Cambridge University Press, 2009), p. 104.

18 Hume, *A Treatise of Human Nature*, p. 662 ('An Abstract').

19 Ibid., pp. 102–3.

20 Ibid., p. 104.

21 Ibid., p. 117.

22 David Hume, *An Enquiry concerning Human Understanding*, in *Enquiries concerning Human Understanding and Concerning the Principles of Morals*, 3rd edn, ed. L. A. Selby-Bigge and P. H. Nidditch (Oxford: Clarendon Press, 1975), pp. 35–36 (IV.ii). See also *Treatise*, pp. 91, 134.

23 Hume, *A Treatise of Human Nature*, p. 134.

24 Hume, *Enquiry concerning Human Understanding*, pp. 44–45.

25 Ibid., pp. 125, 105.

26 Spinoza, *Ethics*, E5P10.

27 Ibid., E5P10, scholium.

28 Ibid., E5P11.

29 Ibid., E1P16

30 René Descartes, *Meditations on First Philosophy*, trans. John Cottingham (Cambridge: Cambridge University Press, 1986), p. 43 (Fourth Meditation).

31 *The Correspondence between Princess Elisabeth of Bohemia and René Descartes*, trans. Lisa Shapiro (Chicago: University of Chicago Press, 2007), p. 92.

32 Ibid., pp. 113–14.

33 Kant describes Humean custom or habit (*Gewohnheit*) as a 'subjective necessity'; see *Critique of Practical Reason*, in Mary Gregor (ed.), *Immanuel Kant: Practical Philosophy* (Cambridge: Cambridge University Press, 1996), p. 181 (V, 51).

34 Hume, *A Treatise on Human Nature*, p. 167 (I.iii.14).

35 Gilles Deleuze, *Empiricism and Subjectivity*, trans. Constantin V. Boundas (New York: Columbia University Press, 1991), p. 66. On this point Deleuze follows Bergson, who writes of 'the habit of contracting habits' in *The Two Sources of Morality and Religion*.

36 G. W. Leibniz, *Discourse on Metaphysics*, art. 7, in *Philosophical Texts*, trans. R. S. Woolhouse and Richard Francks (Oxford: Oxford University Press, 1998), pp. 58–59.

37 G. W. Leibniz, 'Annotatiuncula ad tolandi librum' (on Toland's *Christianity not Mysterious*), in *Opera omnia*, ed. L. Dutens (Geneva: Fratres de Tournes, 1768), vol. 5, p. 144–45.

38 Hume, *Enquiry concerning Human Understanding*, p. 43; Thomas Reid, *Essay on the Active Powers of Man* (Edinburgh, 1788), p. 120.

39 Félix Ravaisson, *Of Habit*, trans. Clare Carlisle and Mark Sinclair (London: Continuum, 2008), p. 39.

40 Ibid., p. 77. On the spiral image in Ravaisson's philosophy, see François Laruelle, *Phénomène et difference: Essai sur l'ontologie de Ravaisson* (Paris: Klincksieck, 1971).

41 Henri Bergson, *The Creative Mind*, trans. Mabelle L. Andison (New York: Philosophical Library, 1946), pp. 231–32.

42 C. S. Peirce, 'A Guess at the Riddle', in *The Essential Peirce: Selected Philosophical Writings*, ed. Nathan Houser and Christian J. W. Kloesel (Bloomington: Indiana University Press, 1992), p. 277.

43 William James, *Psychology: Briefer Course* (Cambridge, MA: Harvard University Press, 1984), p. 125. James's materialist view of habit echoes Hobbes, who argues that habits are '[not] observed in living creatures only, but also in bodies inanimate. For we find that when the lath of a cross-bow . . . remain a long time bent, it will get such a habit, that when it is loosed and left to its own freedom, it will not only not restore itself, but will require as much force for the bringing of it back to its first posture, as it did for the bending of it at first.' See Thomas Hobbes, *Elements of Philosophy, the First Section: Concerning Body*, in *The English Works of Thomas Hobbes*, vol. 4, ed. William Molesworth (London: J. Bohn, 1839), pp. 349–50 (III.xxii.20).

44 Émile Boutroux, *The Contingency of the Laws of Nature*, trans. Fred Rothwell (Chicago and London: Open Court, 1916), p. 192.

45 In chapter 3 of his *Zoological Philosophy*, Lamarck writes that 'every species has derived from the action of the environment in which it has long been placed the *habits* which we find in it. These habits have themselves influenced the parts of every individual in the species, to the extent of modifying those parts and bringing them into relation with the acquired habits.' Darwin makes frequent reference to 'inherited habit' in *The Descent of Man*, and even in *On the Origin of Species* he states that 'There can be little doubt that use in our domestic animals strengthens and enlarges certain parts, and disuse diminishes them; and that such modifications are inherited.' See Charles Darwin, *On the Origin of Species by Means of Natural Selection*, ed. Joseph Carroll (Peterborough, ON: Broadview Press, 2003), pp. 573, 103.

46 Samuel Butler, *Life and Habit* (London: Jonathan Cape, 1924), pp. 298, 300.

47 Butler, *Life and Habit*, p. 51.

48 Butler, *Life and Habit*, p. 50.

49 See, for example, Rupert Sheldrake, *The Science Delusion* (London: Coronet, 2012).

50 Deleuze, *Empiricism and Subjectivity*, p. 85.

51 Ibid., pp. 92–93.

52 Ibid., p. x

53 Deleuze, *Difference and Repetition*, trans. Paul Patton (London: Athlone, 1995), p. 95.

54 Ibid., pp. 94–95.

55 Ibid., p. 96.

56 Ibid., p. 90.

57 Ibid., pp. 95–96.

58 Gilles Deleuze and Félix Guattari, *What Is Philosophy?*, trans. Graham Burchell and Hugh Tomlinson (New York: Columbia University Press, 1996), p. 149. On Deleuze's construal of a concept, see A. E. Moore, *The Evolution of Modern Metaphysics: Making Sense of Things* (Cambridge: Cambridge University Press, 2012), p. 574.

Three

LIFE OR DEATH?

Although our susceptibility to habit is shared in common with other living things, we alone can reflect on and modify the force of habit itself. Perhaps our freedom will consist in this, rather than in complete emancipation from habit. In human life it becomes possible to ask about how habit can best be managed, or utilized, or maybe even transformed in the effort to live well. The good life is not for us merely a matter of self-preservation, of longevity, and therefore the 'life' in question here is something more than biological survival. And there are different senses of this 'something more', to which correspond different ways of being 'good'. We might, for example, say that we 'feel alive', or 'like death', thus drawing attention to the quality of our experience. Or we might reflect on the vitality of our inner life or our spiritual life – and it is here that the duplicity of habit becomes particularly significant. Hegel expresses one aspect of this ambivalence:

> Habit is often spoken of disparagingly and called lifeless, casual and particular. And it is true that . . . it is the habit of living which brings on death, or, if quite abstract, is death itself: and yet habit is indispensable for the *existence* of all intellectual life in the individual, enabling . . . the

matter of consciousness, religious, moral, etc., to be his as this self, this soul, and no other, and be neither a latent possibility, nor a transient emotion or idea, nor an abstract inwardness, cut off from action and reality, but part and parcel of his being.[1]

Proust offers another version of this idea: although he describes habit as a 'deadening force', he acknowledges that it can have the opposite effect. For example, his narrator Marcel observes that the actress Berma is able, with the help of habit, to perform as Phèdre even when she is ill and dying. Marcel finds her 'as extraordinarily charged with life on the stage as she seemed to be moribund if you met her off it.' 'And indeed,' he reflects, 'our habits enable us to a large degree, enable even the organs of our bodies, to adapt themselves to an existence which at first sight would appear to be utterly impossible.'[2] Hegel and Proust may be pointing to different kinds of vitality, and different measures of value, but in each case habit seems to have two contrary effects.

Ambivalence toward habit runs through diverse accounts of the good life. The question of whether living well means being a good person, or having a good time, marks the distinction between what Kierkegaard calls the ethical and aesthetic spheres of existence. From an aesthetic perspective, the pursuit of pleasure provides the dominant criterion of value, the horizon of existential meaning. Of course, effort and even pain – exertion, tension, a tedious wait – may be judged worthwhile for the sake of some pleasures. The aesthetic life can be complex and profound. But it rests on the principle that life is wasted when we miss opportunities for enjoyment, and is fulfilled by the richness, diversity and pleasantness of our experiences. Within the ethical sphere, by contrast, 'good' is a moral category, and happiness is inseparable from virtue. Here, aesthetic considerations are present alongside others: these may be more or less important, but they are not the horizon of concern.

For Kierkegaard himself, neither of these conceptions of the good life is adequate, for it is only in the religious sphere – where a person's relationship to God is both the ground and the task of her existence – that genuine happiness and freedom can be found. While religious existence forms a spherical whole – a consequence of our finitude – it includes conceptions of infinity and eternity, and is characterized by orientation to a source and measure of goodness that transcends any human horizon. (This is just one of the ways in which the religious sphere is, for Kierkegaard, paradoxical.) From this perspective, human existence is not self-sufficient. The person living in the religious sphere recognizes that she is constituted in *essence* by her relationship to God, and so she neither sees nor evaluates herself as an autonomous individual. For reasons both existential and theological, the religious life is qualitatively different from aesthetic and ethical life. In this chapter, then, we will examine the influence of habit from aesthetic and ethical perspectives, and in the following chapter we will turn to its religious significance.

THE PURSUIT OF PLEASURE

From an aesthetic point of view, the decline of sensations that are prolonged or repeated already points to a superficial ambivalence, for habit lessens both pleasure and pain. This is a simple physiological fact, for sensation is the sign of a change, a difference – and it is this difference that is diminished by habit. As Bichat observes, 'The more we look at an object, the less we are sensible of its painful or agreeable qualities ... Every time we see an object, hear a sound, or taste a dish, etc., we find less difference between what we experience and what we have experienced ... Every state of relative pleasure or pain is incessantly brought to a state of indifference by the influence of habit.'[3]

It might be argued, then, that habit has no intrinsic value, one way or the other, for the evaluation of habit is based solely on the nature of the sensations in question: the effects of habit are desirable in the case of painful sensations and undesirable in the case of pleasant ones. As Hegel points out, 'the form of habit, like any other, is open to anything we happen to put into it.' However, Bichat's claim that habit produces 'indifference' suggests otherwise, for this very indifference can be regarded either positively or negatively – and here we are evaluating habit itself. If habit diminishes and flattens experience, then it reduces, quite literally, our feeling of being alive. Insofar as our capacity for experience is valuable in itself, habit seems to be an impoverishing force, even when it makes us less susceptible to pain. On the other hand, habit might temper the intensity of sensations in useful ways: it can prevent us from becoming tired or stressed through overstimulation, for example. Indeed, it sometimes seems that habit itself produces feelings both pleasant and unpleasant: it can be comforting and restful, or it can engender boredom and restlessness.

Again, we can turn to Proust for observation of this ambivalence. In *Time Regained*, the final volume of *In Search of Lost Time*, Marcel describes 'that sensation of extraordinary physical comfort' experienced in a familiar place. Driving through the badly paved streets around the Champs-Élysées, it seems as if the car 'rolls more easily, more softly, without noise, because the gates of a park have been opened and one is gliding over alleys covered in fine sand.' Materially, nothing like this has happened, but, Marcel tells us, 'I felt suddenly that all external obstacles had been eliminated, simply because I no longer had to make that effort of adaptation or attention which we make, sometimes without being conscious of it, in the presence of new things.'[4] A few pages later, however, he describes the 'lively pleasure' he feels 'on every occasion when I find myself torn from my habits – in a new place, or going out at an unaccustomed hour.'[5]

Our productivity as a species testifies to our insatiable desire for the new: new clothes, new recipes, new art, new technologies, new philosophies. The creativity fuelling this perpetual innovation appears to undermine the idea that we are creatures of habit. But, on the contrary, it is habit that drives our search for novelty and spurs our creative work: it is *because* repetition reduces sensation that difference is not only a welcome element of experience, but the very condition of experience. It is, for example, the influence of habit that helps to explain the restless change in fashions from season to season, for we cease to notice colours, shapes and textures once we have become accustomed to them. This phenomenon is intellectual as well as sartorial: fashions may change more slowly in philosophy departments than on the high street, but nevertheless philosophical ideas, vocabularies and styles rise and fall in waves – although they can also become entrenched in individuals who remain faithful to a certain period of thought, like those women who continue through decades to wear the make-up and hairstyles of their youth. Our interest and desire – and our willingness to spend money – are maintained only when we are continually stimulated by novelty. Similarly, habit accounts for the appeal of holidays:

they meet our need not only for rest but for refreshment and reinvigoration. Far from being opposed to habit, then, our desire for difference is inseparable from it – but this desire is nevertheless a kind of resistance or retaliation in the face of habitual indifference.

However, novelty can also be very uncomfortable – even when the change in question is desirable. In the second volume of In Search of Lost Time, Marcel is distressed on the first night of his stay at the luxurious Grand Hotel in Balbec. Although his room is comfortable and pleasant, he cannot relax: his perceptions remain 'on the permanent footing of a vigilant defensive' in this strange and indifferent place, 'full of things which did not know me.' Unable to sleep, he is 'tormented' by the ticking clock, the violet curtains, the glass-fronted bookcases. As this example shows, it is when habit breaks down – or rather, when a change of scene or of circumstance renders our habits redundant – that its significance comes clearly into view.

Such is the force of habit, though, that this disruption is overcome by the development of new habits, which domesticate an unfamiliar place: 'Habit! That skilful but slow-moving arranger [Aménageuse] who begins by letting our minds suffer for weeks on end in temporary quarters, but whom our minds are none the less only too happy to discover at last, for without it, reduced to their own devices, they would be powerless to make any room seem habitable.'[6] Here, the process of re-habitation is depicted as slow and gradual, but elsewhere Proust suggests that habit moves swiftly. During his first night in Balbec, Marcel finds that 'Habit [is] even now setting to work to make me like this unfamiliar lodging, to change the position of the mirror, the shade of the curtains, to stop the clock.'[7] And indeed, if more than a little time were needed for this work, there would be no pleasure in short trips or holidays. Even during a week away one finds a regular haunt: the café one returns to each morning, the table by the window in the local bar for the early-evening Martini. And these temporary habits are a real source of joy, for in combining the novel with the familiar they provide the best of both worlds: they make one feel at home in a new place.

In recommending the cultivation of 'brief habits', Nietzsche elevates this occasional circumstance into a principle of living: 'I love brief habits and consider them an inestimable means for getting to know many things and states, down to the bottom of their sweetness and bitterness.'[8] When a new habit arrives, he admits, 'I always believe that here is something that will give me lasting satisfaction . . . ; and now it nourishes me at noon and in the evening and spreads a deep contentment all around itself and deep into me so that I desire nothing else . . . But one day its time is up; the good thing parts from me, not as something that has come to nauseate me, but peacefully, and as sated with me as I am with it.' And the cycle continues: 'Even now' – as the old habit departs – 'something new is waiting at the door, along with my faith– this indestructible fool and sage! – that this new discovery will be just right, and that this will be the last time. That is what happens to me with dishes, ideas, human beings, cities, poems, music, doctrines, ways of arranging the day, and life styles.' Although this movement from one brief habit to another involves self-deception, Nietzsche regards it as a solution to the dilemma posed by habit:

> Enduring habits I hate. I feel as if a tyrant had come near me and as if the air I breathed had thickened when events take such a turn that it appears that they will inevitably

give rise to enduring habits; for example, owing to an official position, constant association with the same people, a permanent domicile, or unique good health ... Most intolerable, to be sure, and the terrible *par excellence* would be for me a life entirely devoid of habits, a life that would demand perpetual improvisation. That would be my exile and my Siberia.[9]

On this last point, Nietzsche's view is endorsed by William James, who writes that 'there is no more miserable human being than one in whom nothing is habitual but indecision, and for whom the lighting of every cigar, the drinking of every cup, the time of rising and going to bed every day, and the beginning of every bit of work, are subjects of express volitional deliberation.'[10]

While the holidaymaker has a home to return to, and perhaps a constant companion, the way of life that Nietzsche advocates here is radically nomadic. It involves the refusal of what is often regarded as essential to the good life: an occupation, a family, a stable home, lasting good health. This extreme solution to the duplicity of habit is impractical for most of us – we would need to have a private income not only to provide for basic needs, but to allow access to the kind of new habits that Nietzsche finds fulfilling. From an ethical point of view, praising brief habits seems little more than an idealization of faddiness, inconsistency and irresponsibility – as if a toddler exemplified the *summum bonum*. This critique is made explicit in Kierkegaard's *Either/Or* (1843), which dramatizes the aesthetic and ethical ways of life. In this text a young aesthete known as 'A' (his namelessness indicates his refusal of constancy) is criticized for his lack of commitment and earnestness by Judge William, who represents the ethical point of view. Indeed, Kierkegaard's portrayal of 'A' suggests that his way of living is not just ethically reprehensible, but self-defeating even on its own terms: 'A' is perpetually dissatisfied, for his pursuit of entertainment leads to boredom and his pursuit of happiness leads to despair.

The aesthete's approach to life seems to anticipate Nietzsche's recommendation of brief habits: he is a serial seducer who seeks pleasure and stimulation in novel experiences – new people, places, ideas and so on. 'Guard against friendship . . . Never become involved in marriage (for through marriage one falls into a very deadly continuity with custom) . . . Never take any official post,' counsels the aesthete.[11] Complaining that 'habit and boredom have gained the upper hand', and asserting that 'boredom' – rather than idleness – 'is the root of all evil', he suggests an experimental ethic of 'crop rotation', which involves systematic variation. However, closer examination of this idea suggests that the aesthete is advocating something quite different from the Nietzschean principle of 'brief habits'.

Kierkegaard's aesthete distinguishes between extensive and intensive 'crop rotation'. It is the extensive version that resembles Nietzsche's view:

> One is weary of living in the country and moves to the city; one is weary of one's native land and goes abroad; one is weary of Europe and goes to America, etc.; one indulges in the fanatical hope of an endless journey from star to star. Or there is another direction, but still extensive. One is weary of eating on porcelain and eats on silver; wearying on that, one eats on gold; one burns down half of Rome in order to envisage the Trojan conflagration.[12]

According to the aesthete, 'this rotation of crops is the vulgar, inartistic rotation and is based on an illusion . . . this method cancels itself.' The wiser course, he suggests, is to follow the advice of the emperor Antoninus: 'You can begin a new life. Only see things afresh as you used to see them. In this consists the new life.' This points the way to the intensive version of 'crop rotation' that the aesthete recommends. Following the agricultural analogy, this involves changing the method of cultivation, instead of changing the soil. While extensive rotation involves a 'spurious infinity' of variables, intensive rotation relies on limitation. This, argues the aesthete, produces great resourcefulness: he points to the ingenious means of entertainment found by bored school children or by prisoners, who might find amusement in catching a fly or listening to a monotonous dripping from the roof. 'The more resourceful one can be in changing the method of cultivation, the better,' advises the aesthete, 'but every particular change still falls under the universal rule of the relation between recollecting and forgetting.' His explanation of this point is rather cryptic, but what seems to be essential here is the quality of one's attentiveness. He advocates becoming a 'meticulous observer', and suggests that 'one must be very much aware of how one lives, especially of how one enjoys.'

These remarks suggest an alternative to Nietzsche's solution to the problem of habit. A clearer account of this possibility might be developed on the basis of the double law of habit that was first identified by Joseph Butler, and crystallized by Ravaisson. When we reflect on this double law with the question of life's aesthetic value in mind, we see that it complicates habit's effects on pleasure and pain. If habit not only reduces feeling but strengthens and refines activity, then the effects of repetition become less uniform than we have so far acknowledged. Of course, just as habit's dulling of both pleasant and unpleasant sensations indicates a basic ambivalence that does not belong to habit as such, so our attitude to the effects of active habit will depend on the desirability of the action in question. Again, this does not tell us much about habit itself. It is when habit exerts its influence on a complex activity that combines activity and passivity, movement and feeling, that the evaluative question becomes most interesting.

In *De l'habitude* Ravaisson discusses the example of two drinkers: the drunkard (or, alternatively, a casual drinker) and the connoisseur. The first drinker tastes his wine less and less as he continues to drink, but the connoisseur develops a refined palate that makes him increasingly discerning. 'The sensations in which we seek only pleasure soon fade,' writes Ravaisson: 'Taste becomes more and more obtuse in the one who, by passion, is delivered over to the frequent use of strong liquors; in the connoisseur who discovers flavours, it becomes more and more delicate and subtle.'[13] He explains this variation by appealing to the double law of habit. In both cases, drinking involves a combination of action and sensation: holding the glass and feeling its surface; lifting the glass and feeling sensations in the arm; opening the mouth and tasting the wine. For the habitual drunk, however, it is passivity that dominates this particular experience: he is not paying much attention to drinking, perhaps because he is talking to the barman or watching the television, or perhaps because he is simply absent-minded. For the connoisseur, drinking is primarily active: he is attending to the sensations in his mouth and making judgements about the flavours he perceives. In this case, sensation becomes so pervaded by activity that it is intensified by repetition. Of course, the same effects could be observed in comparable situations: the music critic who listens to a song, the masseuse who feels for tension in her client's back, the painter who watches sunlight moving on the sea.

This phenomenon points to a distinction between two kinds of habit, and we shall see that this distinction has important implications within all three 'spheres of existence'. On the one hand, there is ordinary habit, which exemplifies quite straightforwardly Butler's double law: in particular, it is marked by a decline in sensation and a flattening of experience. This certainly has its benefits, for it frees our attention for other things, and – as Proust's narrator learns to appreciate – it makes our environment hospitable. On the other hand, there are circumstances in which the usual effects of habit are modified by a change in attitude. Attentiveness is particularly significant here. A shift in the focus and quality of attention can transform the effects of repetition to engender a heightening of experience rather than a diminution of feeling. This does not transgress the double law of habit; rather, it indicates that sensing has been turned into an activity, so that the law of active habit has greater effect than the law of passive habituation.

We might wonder whether this second phenomenon should also be called habit. William James claims that 'habits depend on sensations not attended to',[14] implying that when sensations *are* attended to then we have left the domain of habit. This is an important insight, and it may make sense to say that the difference between the casual drinker and the connoisseur points to a distinction between habit and practice. Unlike ordinary habit, practice involves attentiveness, and perhaps also choice, effort, and perseverance. (We will return to this later.) But both habit and practice involve continuity and repetition, and combine activity and passivity, movement and feeling – and their effects are equally subject to the double law of habit.

For this reason, the distinction between them can remain internal to the concept of habit. This means that practice should be regarded as an elevation of habit rather than a departure from it. It also suggests that the distinction between the ordinary and the elevated forms of habit signifies an enlargement of habit that seems to be a special feature of human life.

The example of the connoisseur described by Ravaisson helps to clarify the method of intensive 'crop rotation' proposed by Kierkegaard's aesthete. Is it possible to become a connoisseur of experience itself – even of life itself? This would involve a selective intensification of experience by directing and refining one's attention in certain ways. Such a life would combine vitality, discrimination, and good taste, and achieving this would require effort, discipline and purposefulness. In elevating ordinary habit to a principled practice, it would bring into the aesthetic domain elements more usually associated – at least in philosophical discourse – with ethical life. Indeed, this is a path that may lead far beyond the aesthetic sphere delimited by Kierkegaard, for the cultivation of attentiveness is a cornerstone of meditative and contemplative practices. In a religious context, the enrichment of experience at all levels, including the aesthetic, can be a consequence of such practices.

Even within the aesthetic sphere, it is possible to conceive a pure practice of attentiveness and discrimination directed to the intensification of experience. However, more commonly this intensification is mediated through art, which, according to Proust, 'means awareness of our own life'. 'Our habits have long been at work,' he continues, 'and it is the task of art to undo this work of theirs.'[15] Cinema is perhaps most capable of this, since the moving camera aestheticizes, and thus draws attention to, the subjectivity of sensing and experiencing as well as the content of experience. We may feel, on leaving the cinema – at least after a certain kind of film – that we are entering a new world, since our sensitivity is temporarily heightened. This echoes the intensification that happens in times of crisis. I, for example, still vividly remember the bright May morning following the death of my mother, and this memory is less of an inward feeling than of pink blossom against a blue sky, the sound of birdsong, the sensations of air on my face and the pavement beneath my feet as I walked my usual route to school. Proust, for whom art is the most potent method of cleansing the doors of perception, describes how literature can have this kind of effect: 'Certain novels are like great but temporary bereavements, abolishing habit, bringing us back into contact with the reality of life, but for a few hours only, like a nightmare, since the force of habit, the oblivion it creates, the gaiety it restores through the powerlessness of the brain to fight against it and to re-create the truth, infinitely outweigh the almost hypnotic suggestion of a good book which, like all such influences, has very transient effects.'[16]

It is true that suspensions of habit are generally short-lived, but nevertheless Proust's own writing also suggests a more profound alteration – and here the analogy to bereavement is even closer, since there really is a transformation of the world, as happens when we lose those we love most. Marcel describes in detail how the novels of Bergotte and the paintings of Elstir not only refresh his perceptions, but permanently change his way of seeing the world by bringing to his attention elements of experience that hitherto went unnoticed. He finds a similar kind of refreshment in conversation with people of original intelligence and refined sensitivity, such as Swann and Charlus. And, indeed, Proust's novel combines these means of delivery from habit, since it brings the reader into contact with these exceptional conversationalists (including, of course, Marcel) while re-presenting nature, society, art, literature and experience itself in a new and intensified light.

PROUST: HABITS OF THE HEART

Proust is especially interested in the influence of habit on the human heart. It is in a letter to his girlfriend Albertine that Marcel writes, 'As you have told me often, I am first and foremost a man of habit.'[17] Just as repetition and familiarity cause sensations to decline, so they can dull the more complex feelings involved in romantic love. Of course, the 'honeymoon period' of a relationship can last several months (and much longer if the couple are prevented by distance or other circumstances from being together continuously) – and this period is often characterized by a sensual intensity like that produced by art or by crisis. From the perspective of a new relationship, the whole world is refreshed. However, many couples will find that, as Kierkegaard warns, 'love is dissipated in the lukewarmness and indifference of habit.'[18] In this context, the effects of habit have both aesthetic and ethical implications. The inclination to seek relief from habit by taking a holiday or varying one's diet becomes less innocuous when transposed to human relationships, where the 'significant other' is not just a source of sensual pleasure and pain, but also a sensitive subject of experience. In romantic relationships the ethic of crop rotation implies either serial monogamy or serial infidelity. Although in Either/Or Judge William disapproves of the aesthete's general attitude to life, the latter's immorality consists chiefly in his cynical attitude to seduction and his rejection of marriage. Of course,

Kierkegaard's distinction between extensive and intensive crop rotation applies here as in other aspects of the aesthetic life. Judge William can appeal to the aesthete's own theory in arguing that marriage not only enables husbands and wives to find ethical fulfilment in the duties and commitments demanded by their roles, but provides the restriction necessary for resourceful pursuits of pleasure.

Proust argues that habit is 'bound by a diversity of laws', and through the experience of romantic love his narrator discovers new aspects of habit. He suggests that desire can be born of habit, contrary to the more usual view that habit transforms intense desire into dull routine. Swann, who is initially indifferent to Odette, falls in love with her and comes to need her – a pattern that prefigures Marcel's relationship with Albertine. Proust notes that the development of a romantic habit illustrates Hume's philosophical argument that the idea of 'necessary connexion' between two objects is produced by a subjective process of habituation. It is by forming certain ties of association that Marcel comes to fixate on Albertine. Looking back on the relationship, he recognizes the contingency of his love for her: when they met at Balbec he was attracted to the group of friends to which she belonged, and might easily have settled his attention on one of the other girls. 'But gradually, by dint of living with Albertine, I was no longer able to fling off the chains which I myself had forged,' he writes. 'The habit of associating Albertine's person with the sentiment which she had not inspired made me none the less believe that it was peculiar to her, as habit gives to the mere association of ideas between two phenomena, according to a certain school of philosophy, the illusory force and necessity of a law of causation.'[19] In cases like those of Marcel and Albertine, Swann and Odette, a small degree of interest and desire persuades a man to accept a woman's invitations and to receive her visits; the accumulated hours spent together gradually form a habit; and this habit begets a needy, possessive desire. For this reason, writes Proust, 'a woman who is "our type" is seldom dangerous, she is not interested in us' – precisely because we show our interest in her too eagerly – 'she gives us limited contentment and then quickly leaves us without establishing herself in our life, and what on the contrary, in love, is dangerous and prolific of suffering is not a woman herself but her presence beside us every day and our curiosity about what she is doing every minute: not the beloved woman, but habit.'[20]

There seems little reason to derive a general principle from a particular experience, as Proust does here. Indeed, the repetition of this type of love affair for both Swann and Marcel may itself be due to habit, rather than to a universal rule. It is not clear whether Marcel learns his way of being (and especially his way of being in love) from Swann, who was a friend of his parents, or whether his interest in Swann as a boy is due to an affinity he already feels with the older man. As a child, Marcel's obsessive manner of loving is evident in his intense need for his mother's goodnight kiss – that is to say, for her exclusive physical presence – every evening. Proust's novel traces this pattern of emotional dependency through the lives of both characters, and in his later years Marcel reflects on its recurrence:

> Even if one love has passed into oblivion, it may determine the form of the love that is to follow it. Already, even in the midst of the previous love, daily habits existed, the origin of which we did not ourselves remember; perhaps it was a moment of anguish early on

that had made us passionately desire, then permanently adopt, like customs the meaning of which has been forgotten, the habit of those homeward drives to the beloved's door, or her residence in our home, our presence or the presence of someone we trust during all her outings. All these habits, which are like great uniform high-roads along which our love passes daily and which were forged long ago in the volcanic fire of an ardent emotion, nevertheless survive the woman, survive even the memory of the woman.[21]

Here, it is habit that provides a mould – because it opens up a 'high road' or pathway – into which the fluid substance of successive relationships is poured, and settles. Although the mould shared by Swann and Marcel is not universal, there is nevertheless truth in Proust's observation that habit creates attachment, and is therefore 'dangerous and prolific of suffering' – for this happens whether a relationship is formed out of passion or acquiescence in the first place.

Both Marcel and Albertine, like Swann and Odette before them, experience the suffering of habit during their relationship. Even though Marcel is perpetually unsure of his own feelings for Albertine, his doubt about her desire for him causes an anxiety that he seeks to assuage by keeping her with him continually. Inwardly he is in bondage to his habit and the need it has generated, and this results in a literal imprisonment that curtails Albertine's freedom as well as his own. While she is held captive in his house or under the surveillance of a servant, he is unable to travel as he wishes for fear of what she might do in his absence. This, indeed, is another aspect of the ethical consequences of habit in the sphere of personal relationships: it may result in the denial of the other's freedom. And, ironically, this can render the beloved incapable of the love that the possessive person wants to secure.

However, it is when Albertine finally leaves Marcel that he discovers the sharp edge of habit's 'immense force'.[22] He had more or less decided to end the relationship himself, believing that he no longer needs or wants her. But Albertine's departure is the occasion of a revelation: 'I had been mistaken in thinking that I could see clearly into my own heart. But this knowledge, which the shrewdest perceptions of my mind would not have given me, had now been given to me, hard, glittering, strange, like a crystallised salt, by the abrupt reaction of pain.' Marcel now understands not only his own feelings, but an effect of habit that has until now remained hidden:

> I was so much in the habit of having Albertine with me, and now I suddenly saw a new aspect of Habit. Hitherto I had regarded it as an annihilating force which suppresses the originality and even the awareness of one's perceptions; now I saw it as a dread deity, so riveted to one's being, its insignificant face so encrusted in one's heart, that if it detaches itself, if it turns away from one, this deity that one had barely distinguished inflicts on one sufferings more terrible than any other and is then as cruel as death itself.[23]

We hear in this passage an echo of Montaigne's description of habit as 'a violent and treacherous schoolmistress' in his essay "Of Custom, and Not Easily Changing an Accepted Law" (1580). Proust's observation that habit has a sneaky way of gaining despotic power repeats Montaigne's claim that habit 'establishes in us, little by little, stealthily, the foothold of her authority; but having by this mild and humble beginning settled and planted it with the help of time, she soon uncovers to us a furious and tyrannical face against which we no longer have the liberty of even raising our eyes.'[24]

Although Proust is describing one of many ways of loving, the experiences of his narrator and of Swann nevertheless exemplify something of the structure of habit itself. Again, we can look to Ravaisson for philosophical analysis of this. Pointing out that habit 'creates a need' for those sensations that are repeated or prolonged, Ravaisson attributes this to the same process by which active habits become spontaneous. Underlying the double law of habit, he argues, is a single force: 'everywhere, in every circumstance, continuity or repetition – that is, duration – weakens passivity and excites activity. But in this story of two agonistic powers there is a common trait, and this trait explains all the rest . . . Continuity or repetition brings about a sort of obscure activity that increasingly anticipates both the impression of external objects in sensibility, and the will in activity.'[25] The 'obscure activity' or 'anticipation' produced by habit is desire, which takes the shape of the repeated sensation or action: it is a particularized desire for this feeling, for this movement. It is the desire for sensation that manifests itself as need. As long as the sensation in question continues, this need will not be felt, which is why Ravaisson describes the 'activity' generated by habit as 'obscure' and even 'secret' – and why Montaigne and Proust emphasize habit's 'stealth' and dissembling 'insignificance'. However, 'as soon as the cause of the sensation disappears, this need manifests itself in worry and wakefulness . . . one's distress and unease reveal an impotent desire within sensibility.'[26]

When habit's 'obscure activity' produces need, the range of one's desire becomes restricted to certain sensations. Similarly, in the domain of action and movement, the particularization that occurs through habit can narrow the range of one's movements to the point of rigidity. For Ravaisson, this is the extreme and pathological end of a wide spectrum of habit: actions that 'gradually degenerate' into compulsive movements, or 'tics', vividly illustrate the principle by which a habitual action becomes 'a tendency, an inclination that no longer awaits the commands of the will but rather anticipates them.'[27] Bergson, by contrast, suggests that all habitual actions degenerate into rigid automatism. While Ravaisson – as we shall see – regards habit as a principle of life, both natural and divine, Bergson sees it as quasi-mechanical. In *Du rire* (1900), his 'essay on the meaning of the comic', Bergson articulates very clearly the negative evaluation of habit that runs through his other philosophical works. 'The truth is that a really living life should never repeat itself,' he writes here: 'Wherever there is repetition or complete similarity, we always suspect some mechanism at work behind the living.'[28]

Bergson argues that human habit is laughable because it represents a kind of betrayal of vitality by the being in whom life should find its highest expression. Analysing the source of humour in facial expressions, gestures, language and character, he repeatedly returns to this thesis: 'Deep-rooted in the comic, there is always a tendency to take the line of least resistance, generally that of habit . . . The attitudes, gestures and movements of the human body are laughable in exact proportion as that body reminds us of a mere machine.'[29] A person's face, he suggests, 'is all the more comic, the more nearly it suggests to us the idea of some simple mechanical action in which its personality would for ever be absorbed. . . . Automatism, *inelasticity*, habit that has been contracted and maintained, are clearly the reasons why a face makes us laugh.'[30]

To illustrate his theory, Bergson describes an unintentionally comic scene in which a public speaker is betrayed by his habits. Here the gap between life and habit is displayed in the disparity between the intelligence of the speaker's discourse and the mindlessness of his bodily movements:

> In [this] public speaker, we find that gesture vies with speech . . . An idea is something that grows, buds, blossoms and ripens from the beginning to the end of a speech. It never halts, never repeats itself . . . But I find that a certain movement of head or arm, a movement always the same, seems to return at regular intervals. If I notice it and it succeeds in diverting my attention, if I wait for it to occur and it occurs when I expect it, then involuntarily I laugh. Why? Because I now have before me a machine that works automatically. This is no longer life, it is automatism established in life and imitating it. It belongs to the comic.[31]

This example helps to show why mimicry and impersonation are inherently funny. Similarly, Bergson explains, the art of caricature consists in representing a person's inclination or tendency, exaggerating it and making it at once visible and fixed. This produces a distortion that reveals to us a person's nature, so that it is paradoxically *true to life* even while it highlights a mere mechanism where creative, spontaneous life should be. Bergson does not mention that this mechanization of human life has a darker side. We see an early expression of this in Chaplin's 1936 movie *Modern Times*, which dramatizes the automatism of human life in industrialized society – and as machines become increasingly ubiquitous in our own daily lives, then perhaps our habits conform more and more to mechanical processes. Handwriting is replaced by typeface, for example; human contact no longer accompanies everyday transactions like buying groceries, booking a holiday, and putting money in the bank. The effects of habit described by Bergson are not just comical, but tragicomic. Indeed, this is another instance of habit's ambivalence. If habit is an involuntary betrayal of life by the living, then – depending on the context – this can provoke either laughter or lament.

However, it seems strange that the same processes of habituation can produce the attachments of romantic love, usually considered a sign of human depth, and the robotic movements of an ossified or downtrodden character, in which vitality comes to be replaced by a non-human principle. Closer examination of these two effects suggests that the mechanization which Bergson finds to be synonymous with habit is in fact a degradation not only of life, but of habit itself. Habit, we have found, rests on the twin conditions of receptivity to change and resistance to change. Both emotional dependency and quasi-mechanical motion are forms of resistance to change. But while the need that becomes manifest in grief or abandonment is itself a feeling which demonstrates sensitivity to the change that has occurred, automatism signals the absence of receptivity. Machines, after all, cannot acquire habits; they are simply programmed to operate in a certain way.[32] And so the human being whose life has degenerated into mechanical routine has lost her plasticity, her responsive nature. Bergson suggests that in such circumstances laughter can have a salutary effect, like a cold shower on a drunk, precisely because it awakens a deadened sensitivity: 'Laughter is, above all, a corrective. Being intended to humiliate, it must make a painful impression on the person against whom it is directed.'[33] But his view that we need to be saved from a morbid descent into habit indicates a false dualism between life's receptivity and habit's resistance, which is often shared by those who see only one side of habit.

THE MORAL LAW

One of the most negative evaluations of habit in the philosophical tradition is proposed by Kant, who, apparently dismissing any distinction between good and bad habits, writes that 'as a rule, all habits are objectionable.' According to Kant, habit 'leads to thoughtless repetition of the very same act (monotony) and so becomes ridiculous.'[34] While Bergson finds cause for laughter in this 'ridiculous' mechanization of life, Kant is less inclined to see the funny side of habit. Firmly rooted in the ethical sphere, he insists that we cannot be moral as long as we act out of habit – and, since our moral capacity is the mark of human dignity, this means that habit undermines the very possibility of the good life.

This judgement is based on a particularly narrow conception of habit, which seems to follow inevitably from the dualistic basis of Kant's philosophy. In dividing human activity into two domains, regulated by two kinds of law – physical laws that order nature, and the 'laws of freedom' to which the will subjects itself – Kant places habit on the wrong side of a division between causal necessity and moral freedom.[35] If habit belongs to natural, embodied life, then it must be separate from the will, which is the only part of us that is free, and so capable of morality. However, while Kant insists that only a good will (as opposed to helpful actions, compassionate feelings, or benevolent inclinations) can properly be called moral, he also suggests that it is our lack of complete freedom that shapes the moral life as we know it. All human beings, argues Kant, experience morality in the form of commands and obligations. But the feeling of being obliged to do something registers our resistance to the moral law, as well as our interest in that law. This can be contrasted with a hypothetical 'holy will', which resides entirely in the domain of freedom: having no inclinations (and no world in which to act), the holy will experiences no resistance to freedom's laws. It is neither commanded nor obligated to be good; it simply is good, spontaneously, and cannot be otherwise.[36] We human beings cannot, Kant insists, 'come into possession of holiness of will . . . with the pure moral law becoming, as it were, our nature.'[37]

In his late work *The Metaphysics of Morals* (1797), Kant distinguishes habit from 'free aptitude': 'An *aptitude* (*habitus*) is a facility in acting and a subjective perfection of *choice*. – But not every such facility is a *free* aptitude (*habitus libertatis*); for if it is a *habit* (*assuetudo*), that is, a uniformity in action that has become a *necessity* through frequent repetition, it is not one that proceeds from freedom, and therefore not a moral aptitude.'[38] This restriction of the concept of habit leads Kant to write, in his *Anthropology from a Pragmatic Point of View* (1798), that habit is 'a physical inner necessitation to continue behaving in the same way we have behaved thus far,' which as such 'deprives even good actions of their moral value.'[39] When we act out of habit, we allow our behaviour to be shaped by past actions and experiences, and thus relinquish our freedom.

It is worth pausing here to consider how Bergson takes up this view of moral habit. In *The Two Sources of Morality and Religion* (1932) he reinterprets the central concepts of Kantian ethics – duty, obligation and even the categorical imperative – in terms of habit: 'an imperative will tend to become categorical in proportion as the activity brought into play, although intelligent, will tend to become instinctive . . . But an activity which, starting as intelligent, progresses towards an imitation of instinct is exactly what we call, in man, a habit.'[40] Bergson follows Ravaisson in finding an analogy between nature and human activity, but while Ravaisson thinks that the whole of nature, including ourselves, is characterized by freedom, Bergson draws a contrast between natural necessity and human freedom. He argues that when, through habit, human life comes to resemble nature, it takes on nature's necessity:

> An organism subject to inexorable laws is one thing, and a society composed of free wills another. But, once these wills are organized, they assume the guise of an organism; and in this more or less artificial organism habit plays the same role as necessity in the works of nature . . . A human community is a collectivity of free beings. The obligations which it lays down, and which enable it to subsist, introduce into it a regularity which has merely some analogy to the inflexible order of the phenomena of life.[41]

Bergson concludes that 'obligation is to necessity what habit is to nature.'[42] Although he qualifies this claim by saying that it is possible to evade moral obligation, but impossible to evade the laws of nature, he argues that most people do not grasp this distinction, and think that 'every law is a command.' This means that habit is a socially conservative force – and Bergson emphasizes its insidious power: 'When [obligation] has become fully concrete, it coincides with a tendency, so habitual that we find it natural, to play in society the part which our station assigns to us. So long as we yield to this tendency, we scarcely feel it. It only assumes a peremptory aspect, like all deep-seated habits, if we depart from it.'[43] In practice, then, he shares Kant's view that habit undermines freedom. The two philosophers differ, of course, insofar as Bergson identifies habit's quasi-necessity with morality, arguing that 'duty is almost always done automatically,' whereas Kant confines morality to a pure (and thus impractical) domain of freedom.

Kant's influential account of morality challenges the tradition of virtue ethics that draws on Aristotle's suggestion that virtue is a *hexis*. Aristotle's moral philosophy itself is vague enough to inspire quite different interpretations. Thomas Aquinas, for example, emphasizes that a *habitus* – the Latin translation of *hexis* – involves rational choice. He follows the *Nicomachean Ethics* on this point, for Aristotle describes virtue as *hexis prohairetike*, and *prohairesis* signifies choice or motivation.[44] But Aquinas develops the idea in a certain direction. While Aristotle refers to *prohairesis* in discussing a specifically moral kind of habit, Aquinas qualifies the concept of habit as such with reference to the will. In the section of the *Summa theologiae* known as the 'Treatise on Habits', he approvingly cites the definition of *habitus* offered by the Islamic scholar Averroes in his commentary on Aristotle's *De anima*: 'a disposition [*habitus*] is something which a man can exercise in action at will.'[45] Aquinas states that animals cannot acquire habits, that habits belong to the soul and not to the body, and that habit is confined to certain powers of the soul. Indeed, he argues that characteristics acquired from frequent usage (*consuetudo*), by mere repetition, should not properly be called habits.[46]

While Kant restricts the concept of habit to mechanical repetition, Aquinas restricts it to human freedom. This suggests that the difference between their evaluations of habit is to some extent terminological, and a consequence of using the word 'habit' to translate both *habitus* (disposition, aptitude) and *consuetudo* or *assuetudo* (custom, association, repeated practice). Of course, it would be silly to attempt a straightforward comparison between two thinkers who are historically and theologically so far apart. Nevertheless, on the question of habit there is some affinity between them: they both distinguish between *habitus* and *consuetudo*, and associate only the former with freedom and moral action. For both Kant and Aquinas, narrowing the scope of the concept of habit excludes a certain kind of repetition from the good life, and in both cases this seems to separate our ethical activity from the rest of nature.

Other developments of the Aristotelian tradition offer an account of habit that is much further from the Kantian view. It is difficult to imagine any philosopher arguing that the good life consists in mechanical repetition of actions that conform to certain ethical rules or principles. But it is possible to recognize continuity between the two senses of 'habit' distinguished by Aquinas and Kant – and Aristotle himself does not emphasize the distinction between *hexis* and *ethos* (terms that are roughly equivalent to the Latin *habitus* and *consuetudo*).[47] If the concept of habit can be expanded to accommodate both senses, this makes it possible to argue that ordinary habit and the freedom that facilitates moral life are not incompatible. Indeed, they may be regarded as intimately linked.

We find a hint of this idea in one of Joseph Butler's philosophical sermons, preached in 1726 at the Rolls Chapel on Chancery Lane. In his third sermon, 'Upon the Natural Supremacy of Conscience', Bishop Butler suggests that 'when virtue is become habitual, when the temper of it is acquired, what was before "confinement" ceases to be so, by becoming choice and delight.'[48] This, of course, expresses the opposite of Bergson's view that habit turns our freedom into a quasi-necessity. The text for Butler's sermon is Romans 2:14: 'For when Gentiles, who do not have the law, by nature do what the law requires, they are a law unto themselves', and he uses the concept of habit to elucidate this idea of a natural or inward law. However, while Paul's letter implies that some Gentiles are innately 'a law unto themselves', Butler is interested in how such a law is acquired. Moral practice, which initially requires us to conform to externally imposed rules (the Ten Commandments, for example), is through habit gradually appropriated, so that it comes to express our own nature.

In other words, active habit creates a 'second nature' that internalizes a moral code, eventually making this inseparable from our inclinations and tendencies to choose in certain ways – from what Aristotle calls our *hexis prohairetike*. Indeed, Butler is here elaborating an important principle of Aristotelian ethics: that genuine virtue is not only appropriate to the situation in question, but appropriate, or natural, to the virtuous person. Such virtue expresses free activity, rather than obedience to an external command. However, in accordance with Romans 2:14, habit can still be called a law: an inward law or principle that is gradually acquired through repetition, but which comes to regulate our actions. As Butler suggests, again echoing Aristotle, 'delight' in exercising our virtue is a sign that this appropriation has been accomplished. Viewed from this perspective, habit is somewhere between the Kantian moral law and the physical laws of nature, for it has its own peculiar kind of givenness. Habit is a law that we give ourselves, not a rule given to us heteronomously, but once this law is established it can become binding on the body as well as on the will. Although habit can transform virtue from an obligation to a pleasure, the reverse can also happen: something initially desirable may become, through habit, a confinement.

It is Ravaisson who works out the philosophical implications of these ideas, in arguing that reflection on habit calls into question dualisms of mind and body, will and nature, freedom and necessity. Habits, he reminds us, develop gradually, beginning with actions that are consciously chosen and then moving, by degrees, closer to automatic, quasi-instinctual inclinations. The process of habit formation thus reveals a continuous spectrum of activity that stretches from reflective choice to unreflective spontaneity. 'Habit is the dividing line, or the middle term, between will and nature,' writes Ravaisson, 'but it is a moving middle term, a dividing line that is always moving, and which advances by an imperceptible progress from one extremity to the other.'[49] This suggests that the laws of freedom and of habit are not, as Kant claims, two distinct orders. Rather, habit is the embodiment and the naturalization of freedom and intelligence: 'the history of Habit represents the return of Freedom to Nature, or rather the invasion of the domain of freedom by natural spontaneity.'[50] For Ravaisson, this reflection on habit has grand ontological implications, since it offers an insight into nature itself:

> The whole series of beings is therefore only the continuous progression of the successive powers of one and the same principle, powers enveloping one another

in the hierarchy of the forms of life, powers which develop in the opposite direction within the progression of habit. The lower limit is necessity – Destiny, as might be said, but in the spontaneity of Nature; the higher limit is the Freedom of the understanding. Habit descends from the one to the other; it brings these contraries together, and in doing so reveals their intimate essence and their necessary connection.[51]

These ideas can be traced to Schelling, who sought in his metaphysics to overcome the dichotomies of Kantian thought by reconciling freedom and nature.[52] But Ravaisson also draws on Butler's analysis of habit in explaining how the moral life exemplifies, more modestly, a continuity between freedom and nature within the human being.

We saw in Chapter 1 that in his *Analogy of Religion* Butler presents the double law of habit as a principle of moral psychology. He points out that the actions which both produce and express virtue are usually motivated, at least in part, by feelings: for example, compassion for another's distress sometimes moves us to act charitably. This means that the contrary effects of habit on activity and passivity work in combination to alter the overall shape of a person's character. Through habit, argues Butler, we become less upset by the suffering of others, but – partly because our emotions are subdued – better able to act effectively to relieve their distress. This contrasts with the common view that 'compassion fatigue' makes us less responsive to suffering. Nevertheless, Butler claims that 'experience confirms' his account of moral habit, 'for active principles, at the very time that they are less lively in perception than they were, are found to be, some how, wrought more thoroughly into the temper and character, and become more effectual in influencing our practice.'[53] Ravaisson finds that this helps to explain Aristotle's view that virtue becomes easier and more pleasurable over time. Citing the *Analogy of Religion*, he writes that repetition 'gradually leads the pleasure of action to replace the more transient pleasure of passive sensibility. In this way, as habit destroys the passive emotions of pity, the helpful activity and the inner joys of charity develop more and more in the heart of someone who does good.'[54]

The decline of sensation in habit affects not just emotional feeling, but also the feeling of effort and resistance that accompanies all activity. It is this latter kind of feeling that makes us aware of our own actions. Ravaisson states as a general principle that 'by repeated or prolonged exercise . . . the consciousness of effort is effaced.'[55] On this point he follows Maine de Biran, who in *L'Influence de l'habitude sur la faculté de penser* describes how 'the impression of effort is singularly weakened by repetition . . . Resistance diminishes progressively . . . As effort or the motor impression weakens and eventually disappears, the movement is executed without consciousness, without will . . . The most common effect of habit is to take away all resistance, to destroy all friction.'[56] By drawing on the discussions of habit presented by both Butler and Maine de Biran, Ravaisson explains this influence of habit in the moral sphere: 'Virtue is first of all an effort and wearisome; it becomes something attractive and a pleasure only through practice, as a desire that forgets itself or that is unaware of itself, and gradually it draws near to the holiness of innocence.'[57]

As a general rule, habit replaces resistance with spontaneity, and when applied to morality this has significant philosophical implications. As we have seen, Kant claims that our resistance to the moral law means that we necessarily encounter this law in the form of obligations, which may of course be unwelcome, tedious, inconvenient. However, Ravaisson is suggesting that habit, in wearing down resistance, provides a bridge to the kind of 'holy will' which, for Kant, remains forever inaccessible to us. Even if we can never become perfectly good, he argues, we can 'draw near' to the spontaneous goodness of a 'holy' being. In this way, habit offers a route to the sanctification that is deemed impossible by Kant. Through habit, virtue becomes less and less an obligation, and increasingly expresses our own nature. This is what Butler already points to when he writes that virtue ceases to be 'confinement' when it becomes habitual, although of course it is Ravaisson who sees how this insight challenges the Kantian view.

In one sense, all this simply elaborates the Aristotelian thesis that moral virtue is 'the child of habit [*ethos*]', which 'ends up as our nature'.[58] But, read in historical context, it responds not only to Kantian moral theory, but to the philosophical basis of Kant's claim that habit and morality are incompatible. Ravaisson, like the German idealists, is proposing a reconciliation of freedom and nature that provides metaphysical support for the idea that moral life can be embedded within both the human body and social institutions. He suggests that forming a '*second nature*' is 'the secret of education': that we should civilize our children by orienting them 'towards the good by action, thus fixing the inclination for it.'[59] This is strikingly similar to Hegel's view that 'education . . . begins with pupils whose life is at the instinctive level and shows them the way to a second birth, the way to change their instinctive nature into a second, spiritual nature, and makes this spiritual level habitual to them.'[60] Hegel develops this Aristotelian insight into an explicit critique of Kant's philosophy when he argues that communal ethical life (*Sittlichkeit*) is 'the concept of freedom developed into the existing world', since 'custom [*Sitte*] is the law appropriate to free mind.'[61] Of course, as Bergson highlights, this kind of view may be politically conservative – and this is where the Kantian critique of habit remains important. By separating human freedom and dignity from forms of life that tend to instantiate injustice, Kant offers a moral perspective from which social institutions, customs and practices can be interrogated.[62]

HABIT AND PRACTICE

Even if we find philosophical reasons for challenging the Kantian division between *consuetudo* and *habitus*, there is nevertheless an important practical difference between the habits we fall into, and those we cultivate. The distinction between ordinary habit and practice that was introduced earlier in this chapter helps to capture the difference between unreflective and reflective habit. A practice is a habit that is consciously and deliberately developed. While Kant suggests that mechanical repetition and free aptitude belong to two separate orders – that of physical causality, and that of the moral law – practice is a kind of habit, and operates in the same way. Both ordinary habit and practice develop through repetition, which influences action and feeling; both are therefore subject to the double law of habit. Moreover, both begin with actions that are chosen, and often attended to, and gradually become spontaneous and effortless. Some of the most compulsive habits start with an effort: few people enjoy their first cigarette or their first alcoholic drink, for example, but have to acquire a taste for them. And some of the noblest practices become entirely unconscious. As Ravaisson puts it, virtue that is thoroughly established produces 'desire that forgets itself', and so resembles 'the holiness of innocence'.

However, we still feel that we fall blindly into ordinary habits, whereas practice involves an explicit decision. And the difference between ordinary habit and practice is certainly significant. It would be simplistic to suggest that this difference is due to choice. Rather, while habit wills a particular action, practice wills the repetition of the action, as both means and end. That is to say, the practitioner chooses to repeat (to practise) in order to cultivate a disposition that will itself generate repeated, consistent activity. The person who practises the piano wants to be a piano player; the athlete wants to excel at her sport. Their desires and decisions are made concrete in their commitment to practice every day. This contrasts with the smoker who does not want to smoke habitually yet desires this cigarette, or the alcoholic who does not choose to drink repeatedly but wants this drink. In the case of practice, the particular actions – musical or athletic exercises, for example – may or may not be desirable for their own sake, but their repetition is desirable, and requires each singular act. Practice takes the mechanism of habit and puts it to a determinate use, to deliberately refashion both the mind and the body. It is thus a specifically human elevation of habit that is, nevertheless, continuous with the habits found throughout the natural world.

According to philosophers like Aristotle, Butler and Ravaisson, moral virtue is a practice in this specific sense – although they do not clarify the distinction between practice and ordinary habit. We tend to fall into habit to avoid effort, to save energy; this applies even when the task in question is quite a complex one, such as dealing with difficult emotions or a demanding social situation (where cigarettes and alcohol can come to the rescue). In contrast, moral virtue is 'first of all an effort, and wearisome', but over time it becomes easy and natural. In other words, it becomes just like habit: apparently mindless, taken for granted, entirely appropriated and thus part of one's 'way of being'. Here, then, we have a single phenomenon that invites contrasting evaluations. For the Kantian, the mindlessness of a 'second nature' renders it neither free nor virtuous. For the Aristotelian thinkers we have considered, this same mindlessness signifies that virtue has, through patient practice, been successfully appropriated.

The distinction between ordinary habit and practice should not imply that the latter has to make its method explicit. On the contrary, practitioners do not need to understand the processes of habit acquisition in order to practise freely and effectively. Even where these processes are codified in training manuals, academic curricula, or programmes of reform, they often remain implicit. It is only in disciplines such as psychology, pedagogy or philosophy that the mechanisms of habit are investigated theoretically – and perhaps it is only in certain spiritual and therapeutic practices that a first-person understanding of these mechanisms becomes part of the process of development and transformation.

Education or training almost always involves practice, and in some cases simply *is* practice. Here, though, one person undergoes a process of habituation that is consciously and deliberately directed by another. A student or trainee may feel that she is blindly going through the motions of a mechanical repetition – and if she is unable to grasp her teacher's purposefulness at all then perhaps this is true. But nevertheless, from the educator's perspective the repetition itself is being willed, and not just each singular instance. According to Aristotle, education has to begin by training the irrational part of a young person's soul to obey reason. It is habit, or rather practice, that effects this training: practice *regulates* the student's desires and emotions so that by the time she is mature enough to learn philosophy, her habits are already properly ordered in conformity with reason. This is why Aristotle, in the *Nicomachean Ethics*, insists on a minimum age for studying moral philosophy.[63]

This account of education can be applied in a religious context. For example, the medieval Islamic thinker Miskawayh, who was influenced by Aristotle via Galen's ethical writings, writes that 'It is the Law [*sharia*] that sets the youth on the straight path, habituates them to admirable actions, and prepares their souls to receive wisdom, to seek the virtues, and to reach human happiness through sound thought and upright reasoning.'[64] Miskawayh, like Galen, insists that habit belongs to the 'bestial soul' rather than to the rational soul. Nevertheless, he says that when a person is old enough to learn wisdom he will recognize the purpose and intelligibility of the Law, which implies that even the irrational aspects of the soul can be ordered according to reason. If practice consists in the rational part of the soul directing the irrational part, then education consists in the rational part of one soul (the teacher's) directing the irrational part of another soul (the student's). There is always a danger, of course, that the teacher's own soul is not properly ordered, and that education will be unenlightened and misdirected. This kind of teaching is indoctrination rather than philosophical education, which, for Aristotle and his followers, has to be oriented to human happiness and fulfilment (*eudaimonia*).

Another variant of practice is the adoption of a daily routine or timetable in order to maximize productivity or creativity. In this case, the self-imposed habit does not aim to cultivate a particular disposition, skill or virtue. Its purpose is to provide a framework that effaces effort and decision about everyday matters: when to get up, what to wear, how to wash, when to eat, and so on. So a writer or an artist, for example, might adopt such a schedule in order to write or to paint with a clear mind. Such habits may be idiosyncratic, for they are usually solitary. But they have a similar effect to the communal routines followed by monks and nuns, who live by a rule designed to free their attention for prayer. As William James observes, 'the more of the details of our daily life we can hand over to the effortless custody of automatism, the more our higher powers of mind will be set free for their own proper work.'[65]

NOTES

1 *Hegel's Philosophy of Mind (Part Three of the Encyclopaedia of the Philosophical Sciences)*, trans. William Wallace and A. C. Miller (Oxford: Clarendon Press, 1971), p. 143 (§410).

2 Marcel Proust, *Time Regained*, vol. 6 of *In Search of Lost Time*, trans. C. K. Scott Moncrieff and Terence Kilmartin, revised by D. J. Enright (London: Vintage, 1996), pp. 383–84.

3 Xavier Bichat, *Physiological Researches on Life and Death*, trans. Tobias Watkins (Philadelphia: Smith & Maxwell, 1809), pp. 34–37.

4 Proust, *Time Regained*, p. 206.

5 Ibid., p. 216.

6 Proust, *In Search of Lost Time*, vol. 1, p. 7.

7 Proust, *In Search of Lost Time*, vol. 2, p. 287.

8 Friedrich Nietzsche, *The Gay Science*, trans. Josefine Naukhoff, ed. Bernard Williams (Cambridge: Cambridge University Press, 2001), p. 167 (§295).

9 Ibid., p. 167.

10 Ibid., p. 168.

11 S. Kierkegaard, Either/Or, vol. 1, trans. Howard V. Hong and Edna H. Hong (Princeton: Princeton University Press, 1987), pp. 295–98.

12 Ibid., pp. 291–92.

13 Félix Ravaisson, Of Habit, trans. Clare Carlisle and Mark Sinclair (London: Continuum, 2008), p. 49.

14 William James, Psychology: Briefer Course (Cambridge, MA: Harvard University Press, 1984), p. 131.

15 Proust, Time Regained, pp. 254–55.

16 Proust, In Search of Lost Time, vol. 5: The Captive/The Fugitive, p. 642.

17 Ibid., p. 519.

18 Søren Kierkegaard, Works of Love, trans. Howard V. Hong and Edna H. Hong (Princeton: Princeton University Press, 1998), p. 36.

19 Proust, Time Regained, p. 576.

20 Proust, In Search of Lost Time, 4: Sodom and Gomorrah, p. 417.

21 Proust, The Captive/The Fugitive, pp. 780–81.

22 Ibid., p. 489.

23 Ibid., p. 478.

24 Michel de Montaigne, 'Of Custom, and Not Easily Changing an Accepted Law', in The Complete Essays of Montaigne, trans. Donald M. Frame (Stanford: Stanford University Press, 1958), p. 77.

25 Ravaisson, Of Habit, pp. 49–51.

26 Ibid., pp. 51–53.

27 Ibid., p. 51.

28 Henri Bergson, Laughter: An Essay on the Meaning of the Comic, trans. Cloudesley Brereton and Fred Rothwell (London: Macmillan, 1913), p. 34. On Bergson's interpretation of habit, see Dominique Janicaud, Ravaisson et le métaphysique: Une généalogie du spiritualisme français (Paris: Vrin, 1997), pp. 39–50; Alexandra Renault, 'L'Habitude chez Bergson: Une esquisse du concept phénoménologique de Stiftung?', Alter 12 (2004): 79–103; Mark Sinclair, 'Is Habit the Fossilised Residue of a Spiritual Activity? Ravaisson, Bergson, Merleau-Ponty', Journal of the British Society for Phenomenology 42, no. 1 (2011): 33–52.

29 Bergson, Laughter, pp. 196; 29.

30 Ibid., p. 25.

31 Ibid., p. 32.

32 John Dewey argues that habit only becomes mindlessly repetitive when it is 'the product of conditions that are uniform because they have been made so mechanically – as in much school and factory "work".' See Logic:

The Theory of Inquiry, in John Dewey: The Later Works, 1925–1953, ed. Jo Ann Boydston (Carbondale: Southern Illinois University Press, 1980), p. 39.

33 Bergson, Laughter, p. 197.

34 Immanuel Kant, Anthropology from a Pragmatic Point of View (1798), trans. Robert B. Louden, in Günter Zöller and Robert B. Louden (eds), Immanuel Kant: Anthropology, History and Education (Cambridge: Cambridge University Press, 2007), p. 261.

35 Immanuel Kant, Groundwork of the Metaphysics of Morals (1785), in Mary Gregor (ed.), Immanuel Kant: Practical Philosophy (Cambridge: Cambridge University Press, 1996), p. 43 (IV, 387). To be more precise, Kant distinguishes between causal necessity and the kind of necessity which belongs to the moral law, which is neither causal nor logical necessity.

36 See Kant, Groundwork, pp. 67, 88 (IV, 414, 439).

37 Kant, Critique of Practical Reason, p. 206 (V, 82).

38 Kant, Metaphysics of Morals, p. 535 (VI, 407). See also pp. 515–16 (VI, 383–85).

39 Kant, Anthropology, p. 261.

40 Henri Bergson, The Two Sources of Morality and Religion, trans. R. Ashley Audra and Cloudesley Brereton (London: Macmillan, 1935), p. 16.

41 Ibid., pp. 1, 3.

42 Ibid., p. 6.

43 Ibid., p. 10.

44 Aristotle, Nicomachean Ethics, trans., ed. Roger Crisp (Cambridge: Cambridge University Press, 2000), pp. 31, 104 (1106b36, 1139a22–23); see also Eudemian Ethics, trans., ed. Brad Inwood and Raphael Woolf (Cambridge: Cambridge University Press, 2013), p. 38 (1227b). On habit in Aristotle's ethics, see Claudia Baracchi, Aristotle's Ethics as First Philosophy (Cambridge: Cambridge University Press, 2008), pp. 66–73, 90–91, 112–22; M. F. Burnyeat, 'Aristotle on Learning to be Good', in Amelie Oksenberg Rorty (ed.), Essays on Aristotle's Ethics (Berkeley and Los Angeles: University of California Press, 1980), pp. 69–92; E. Garver, 'Aristotle's Metaphysics of Morals', Journal of the History of Philosophy 27 (1989): 7–28; Joe Sachs' preface and introduction to his translation of the Nicomachean Ethics (Newbury, MA: Focus Publishing, 2002), pp. vii–xvii; and Nancy Sherman, The Fabric of Character (Oxford: Clarendon Press, 1989), pp. 157–99.

45 Thomas Aquinas, Summa theologiae, vol. 22: Dispositions for Human Acts (Ia2ae 49–54), trans. A. Kenny (Oxford: Blackfriars; and London: Eyre & Spottiswoode, 1964), pp. 16–17 (I-II.49.3). On habit in Aquinas, see Bonnie Kent, 'Habits and Virtues (Ia IIae, qq. 49–70)', in Stephen J. Pope

(ed.), *The Ethics of Aquinas* (Washington, DC: Georgetown University Press, 2002), pp. 116–30. On the continuities between Aristotelian *hexis* and Thomist *habitus*, see also Jean-Luc Marion, *Sur l'ontologie grise de Descartes* (Paris: Vrin, 1975), pp. 25–30.

46 Thomas Aquinas, *Summa theologiae*, vol. 23: *Virtue (Ia2ae 55–67)*, trans. W. D. Hughes (Oxford: Blackfriars; and London: Eyre & Spottiswoode, 1969), p. 33 (I-II.56.5).

47 See Jacques Chevalier, *L'Habitude: Essai de métaphysique scientifique* (Paris: Boivin, 1929), pp. 7–14.

48 Joseph Butler, 'Upon Human Nature', Sermon III, in *Five Sermons*, ed. Stephen L. Darwell (Indianapolis: Hackett, 1983), p. 44.

49 Ravaisson, *Of Habit*, p. 59.

50 Ibid., p. 77.

51 Ibid., p. 67.

52 See Christiane Mauve, 'Ravaisson, lecteur et interprète de Schelling', *Romantisme* 88 (1995): 65–74.

53 Butler, *Analogy of Religion, Natural and Revealed, to the Constitution and Course of Nature* (Oxford: Oxford University Press, 1907), p. 108.

54 Ravaisson, *Of Habit*, p. 69.

55 Ibid., p. 59.

56 Maine de Biran, *The Influence of Habit on the Faculty of Thinking*, trans. Margaret Donaldson Boehm (Westport, CT: Greenwood Press, 1970), pp. 59, 47.

57 Ravaisson, *Of Habit*, p. 69.

58 Aristotle, *Nicomachean Ethics*, pp. 23, 136 (1103a, 1152a).

59 Ravaisson, *Of Habit*, p. 69.

60 G. W. F. Hegel, *Hegel's Philosophy of Right*, trans. T. M. Knox (Oxford: Oxford University Press, 1952), p. 260 (§51, *Zusatz*).

61 *Hegel's Philosophy of Right*, pp. 105–9; 260.

62 There is an important strand of critique in this tradition, which broadens out from philosophy to include history and the social sciences (where Pierre Bourdieu's concept of 'habitus', following Erwin Panofsky, Marcel Mauss, and William James has been influential). See, for example, S. Sullivan, *Revealing Whiteness: The Unconscious Habits of Racial Privilege* (Bloomington: Indiana University Press, 2006). For an overview, see Tony Bennett *et al.*, 'Habit and Habituation: Governance and the Social', *Body & Society* 19, nos. 2 and 3 (2013): 3–29. On the concept of habitus, see Bourdieu's 'Postface' to Panofsky's *Gothic Architecture and Scholasticism*: an English translation of Bourdieu's text is provided in Bruce Holsinger, *The Premodern Condition* (Chicago: University of Chicago Press, 2005), pp. 221–42.

63 Aristotle, *Nicomachean Ethics*, p. 5 (1095a).

64 *Miskawayh: The Refinement of the Soul*, trans. C. Zurayk (Beirut: American
   University of Beirut, 1968), p. 35.

65 James, *Psychology: Briefer Course*, p. 134.

Four

SPIRIT OR FLESH?

The ethical task of developing a certain kind of character, becoming a certain kind of person, is called into question by religious ideas about our inability to fulfil our human potential without divine assistance. Variations on this view are found in most spiritual traditions, although Christianity will be our focus here since it is so intimately connected to the European philosophical tradition. In *The City of God against the Pagans* Augustine argues that classical philosophers like Cicero display a 'wondrous vanity' in seeking 'to achieve blessedness by their own efforts'.[1] Nevertheless, being religious is a certain way of being human, and this means that philosophical accounts of virtue can illuminate the spiritual life. When we consider the question of the good life from a religious point of view, we encounter once again a profound ambivalence towards habit, even when this is considered as a broad concept that encompasses both ordinary habit and practice.

In Christian theology, as in Western philosophy, the concept of habit plays an important role in debates about human freedom. Kant's work makes it clear that the challenge for modern philosophy is to reconcile our intuitive sense of our own freedom with the apparently deterministic force of physical laws. But in a theological context, the task is to maintain a delicate balance between human and divine power. This involves recognizing human freedom – which is presupposed by most Christian teaching – without compromising the equally important belief in a creator God on whom we remain dependent for our continued existence and activity.

The doctrine of original sin further complicates this question of freedom. In Augustine's theology, for example, we encounter the idea that sin, understood as the will's tendency to turn away from God and assert itself independently, prevents us from being the source of our virtue. Moreover, trying to be virtuous through our own actions leads to pride, which is itself the root of sin, so that the effort to be good becomes entirely self-defeating. And on a more psychological note, Augustine suggests that habit (*consuetudo*) only exacerbates the bondage of sin:

> The rule of sin is the force of habit, by which the mind is swept along and held fast even against its will . . . I was held fast, not in fetters clamped upon me by another, but by my own will, which had the strength of iron chains . . . [For desire had grown from my will] and when I gave in to desire habit was born, and when I did not resist the habit it became a necessity . . . These two wills within me, one old, one new, one the servant of the flesh, the other of the spirit, were in conflict and between them they tore my soul apart.[2]

Here Augustine is offering a confessional gloss on Romans 7, where Paul describes an internal conflict between two different kinds of desire, two causal orders: the flesh and the spirit. Augustine finds that after his conversion to true Christianity his habits keep him stuck in his former way of life. One of the interesting things about this passage is that the concept of habit helps Augustine to make sense of the idea of a real bondage for which he is nevertheless responsible – an idea that is, after all, essential to the doctrine of original sin. His habits, he emphasizes, come from his own will, and he is free to 'resist' their development; however, when he fails to do this, these habits become 'a necessity' that constrains him 'against his will'.[3] Like Ravaisson, then, Augustine sees in habit a 'chain' that links freedom and necessity, although he interprets this much more pessimistically.

Just as Augustine finds habit to be both psychologically and theologically significant, so in *De l'habitude* Ravaisson connects the facility and naturalness born of habit with the idea of grace. Characteristically, though, he accentuates continuity rather than opposition between natural and spiritual laws. While Paul's Letter to the Romans describes a conflict between the 'law of the limbs', or the inclinations of the flesh, and the spiritual law, Ravaisson writes that habit 'is, indeed, a law, a *law of the limbs*, which follows on from the freedom of spirit. But this law is a *law of grace*.'[4] In one sense he means this figuratively, suggesting that virtuous behaviour which is initially difficult becomes easy and even effortless, as if an external power has interceded to help a person become good. But in linking habit and grace Ravaisson is also making reference to a theological application of the concept of *habitus* to describe how divine grace is appropriated by human beings.

THE HABIT OF GRACE

Augustine suggests that it is solely through God's grace, and not by our own power, that we can become capable of following the Christian commandment to love both God and one another. This principle remains unchallenged throughout the mainstream theological tradition, and is re-emphasized in Reformation thought. However, the precise manner in which divine grace is bestowed and received has proved a contentious issue. Augustine's view, which dominated Western Christianity for several centuries, is that human beings are turned from sin to virtue by a direct intervention of God, acting in the form of the Holy Spirit. But in the later medieval period Aquinas provided an alternative account of grace, suggesting that it is given as a *habitus* that empowers us to exercise Christian virtue. Although the view that virtue lies innately within us is theologically troublesome for Aquinas, the idea that it comes from the outside is also problematic – for this makes our virtue seem unnatural, the result of an intervention that compromises our freedom too much. Indeed, we might question whether such virtue is really *ours* at all. While the Augustinian tradition – particularly in some of its later developments – emphasizes the corruption of nature and human nature following the fall, Aquinas, accentuating the fundamental goodness of God's creation, finds more continuity between nature and grace. He argues that grace completes and fulfils the natural order, rather than redirecting it from evil to good, as Augustine suggests.

The sense of appropriation that is embedded in the concept of *hexis* or *habitus* – both rooted, of course, in the verb 'to have' – enables Aquinas to explain how divine grace may belong to us. The analogy between moral virtue and Christian virtue suggests that both can become a 'second nature', although by different processes of acquisition: one is cultivated by ethical practice while the other is 'infused' by God. In developing this account of grace Aquinas steers a tricky course between pagan philosophy and Christian tradition. When he defines virtue in the *Summa theologiae* he appeals not to Aristotle's *Ethics* but to Peter Lombard's *Sentences*, then the standard textbook of Christian theology: 'Virtue is a good quality of the mind, by which we live rightly, of which no one makes bad use, which God works in us without us.'[5] But having cited this definition, Aquinas replaces *qualitas* with *habitus*. As we saw in Chapter 1, Aristotle distinguishes the categories of *hexis* and *diathesis* (state or quality) on the grounds that a *hexis* is longer lasting and more stable – and, crucially, has become 'natural', constitutive of a person's way of being. By suggesting that the God-given virtue of love or charity (*caritas*), from which the other Christian virtues follow, should be understood as a *habitus* in precisely this sense, Aquinas revises Lombard's Augustinian view that we act charitably only when directly (and temporarily) moved by the Holy Spirit's action 'in us without us'. He explains that habit 'works in the same way as a nature', and thus 'makes the doing of something our own, as if natural to us, so to speak, and therefore pleasurable.'[6]

If grace is a *habitus* we may not only receive it transiently, but possess it over time. This makes it a genuine gift: divinely infused virtue is properly ours, even though we have not generated it by ourselves. Aquinas's use of the concept of *habitus* also indicates that grace enables us to exercise our virtue *freely*. This makes most sense when we understand human freedom as natural spontaneity rather than reflective choice or 'free will'. As we have seen, spontaneity follows from the habits we acquire ourselves, and Aquinas is suggesting that it similarly follows from a *habitus* infused by God. As in Aristotelian philosophy, this kind of virtue not only brings consequential rewards like friendship and esteem – and, in the Christian context, greater hope of salvation – but also gives pleasure while it is being exercised. Whereas Augustine invokes habit to attribute sinfulness to human freedom, Aquinas invokes it to secure the link between freedom and virtue. This Aristotelian conception of habit helps him to explain why the Christian life is not just morally worthy, and a means to the end of eternal happiness, but also a source of worldly joy.

Aquinas's account of grace as *habitus* was taken up by other scholastic theologians, and this whole way of understanding divine gifts became one of the contentious issues of the Reformation. Luther's radical critique of Church teaching responded to the voluntarism – the excessive emphasis on free will – that he found in late scholastic theology, as well as to institutional corruption and abuses of religious authority. Luther's rejection of the category of *habitus* was due in part to his general hostility to Aristotle, whose philosophy had become almost inseparable from scholasticism. At times, his polemic against 'the Schools' focuses on Aristotle's moral psychology: in 1516 he wrote that 'we are not, as Aristotle believes, made righteous by the doing of just deeds . . . but rather in becoming and being righteous people we do just deeds.'[7] But more particularly, Luther returns to the Augustinian tradition in questioning the idea that grace becomes our own in any enduring sense. Again, Paul's Letter to the Romans provides a theological battleground: in his lectures on this text, Luther contrasts a proud, boastful 'person of the law' who is 'confident in the righteousness which he already possesses' with the 'humble' person of faith who 'prays for the righteousness which he hopes to acquire'. According to Luther, the 'whole life' of faith 'is nothing else but prayer, seeking and begging . . . always seeking and striving to be made righteous . . . never standing still, never possessing.'[8] He is ambiguous on this point, though, for he also suggests that righteousness is 'ours', though 'not by virtue of anything in us, or in our own power.'[9]

Although it is often hard to pin Luther down to a precise doctrinal position, his overall orientation is clear enough. From his theological perspective, conceiving grace as a *habitus* leaves too much room for self-assertion, and allows too much emphasis on good works – ordinary moral behaviour – as a means to salvation. Despite being divinely infused, a *habitus* still requires human action in order to bear fruit, since a disposition to be virtuous has to be exercised, or actualized, by doing good deeds. The gap between potentiality and actuality, implicit in the concept of a disposition, is fertile ground for the idea of spiritual merit that Luther opposes so vehemently. So he finds that the scholastic doctrine of grace permits a connection between works and salvation that is vulnerable to the danger – which Augustine had identified centuries earlier – of pride infecting virtue, and thereby corrupting spiritual practice at its very core. While Aquinas could explain the exercise of a divinely infused *habitus* by appealing to a natural desire for the good which, when empowered by grace, facilitates the Christian life, Luther sees a much sharper contrast between grace and nature. He emphasizes that even our desire for God does not come from ourselves: 'Those who seek God, do good freely and gladly, purely for the sake of God alone . . . But this is the work not of our nature but of grace.'[10] Righteousness, he suggests, 'comes completely from the outside' and is 'foreign' to our nature: 'God does not want to redeem us through our own, but through external, righteousness and wisdom; not through one that comes from us and grows in us, but through one that comes to us from the outside.'[11] Although Aquinas would also deny that virtue 'comes from us', the concept of *habitus* does seem to accommodate the idea that the gift of grace, once planted by God, can 'grow in us'. For Luther, by contrast, the divine gift slips through our fingers as soon as we receive it.

If Ravaisson's description of habit as a 'law of grace' makes reference to this theological debate, it is also possible to draw from his account of habit a way of reconciling the Catholic and Protestant views on grace. Ravaisson understands habit (in the sense of disposition) as not just a capacity but a *tendency* to act in a certain way. In moral habit, he writes, 'repetition or continuity . . . develops within the soul not only the disposition, but also the inclination and tendency to act, just as in the organs it develops the inclination for movement.'[12] This recalls the distinction drawn by Locke and Reid between habit considered as a 'power or ability' and as a 'disposition', which, involving 'an inclination or impulse to do the action', is 'forward', having its own momentum. Developing these ideas, Ravaisson suggests that although the *theoretical* distinction between potentiality and actuality is integral to the concept of a disposition, this difference is, *in practice*, gradually effaced in the acquisition of a habit.[13]

When applied to the Christian doctrine of grace, this dynamic conception of habit – which already seems to be implicit in Aquinas's account of virtue[14] – accommodates the idea that human beings can possess a divine gift once it is given to them, and are even able to cultivate it through their own actions. When love is expressed, it not only extends but intensifies; it is consolidated as well as dispersed. As Ravaisson puts it, 'Love is augmented by its own expressions.'[15] But understanding habit as tendency also avoids the implication that it is entirely up to individuals to actualize the divinely infused *habitus*, since this has its own momentum. This means that someone who receives grace can consider it her own, while remaining aware that it is God's power that moves through her when she is inclined to do good. If grace is given in the form of a *habitus* that includes a tendency to repeat itself, the distinction between divine and human action will be gradually effaced as this tendency becomes a second nature. The philosophical conception of habit as tendency helps to explain Aquinas's view that grace is not simply operative, but co-operative – that God 'acts in us in such a way that we too act.'[16] In this fusion of God's activity with our own, grace repeats itself, augments itself, expresses itself in the world.

KIERKEGAARD: RELIGIOUS REPETITION

Even for those of us untroubled by the metaphysics of grace, this theological discussion indicates how much can be at stake in the concept of habit. It shows that habit bears on questions of freedom, selfhood, identity; it brings to the fore the question of appropriation. And Luther's critique of the scholastic response to these questions is echoed in a different key, three centuries later, in Kierkegaard's critique of Hegelian thought. For these nineteenth-century philosophers – both brought up in the Lutheran tradition – the questions of freedom and appropriation pertain more to the nature of the religious life than to theological doctrine.

We have already seen that Hegel, seeking to overcome the dualisms of Kantian thought, describes custom as a law of freedom: as the embodied and institutional expression of human 'spirit'. For Hegel, as for Kierkegaard, 'spirit' signifies consciousness, purposefulness, and above all freedom. Hegel draws out both Christian and philosophical implications of this concept of spirit when he writes that ethical education teaches people 'the way to a second birth, the way to change their instinctive nature into a second, spiritual nature, and makes this spiritual level habitual to them.'[17] His reference to a 'second birth' alludes to New Testament descriptions of religious conversion or awakening: in John 3, Jesus tells Nicodemus that he must be 'born of the spirit', and similar ideas are found in Paul's letters. Hegel connects this notion of spiritual birth with the Aristotelian idea of a second nature – 'a second, spiritual nature'. He is suggesting here that spirituality should be appropriated through custom and socialization; that the spiritual should be made habitual.

Kierkegaard's entire authorship rages against this inter-pretation of the religious life. Warning of 'the bondage of habit', he suggests that the repetitions of customary practice 'have a diversionary power' that leads people away from authentic faith.[18] Echoing Kant's claim that habit makes us 'ridiculous', Kierkegaard states that 'the most ludicrous thing Christianity can ever become is what is called custom and habit in the banal sense.'[19] Here, in *Concluding Unscientific Postscript* (1846), he argues that 'habit and routine and lack of passion' – a sure sign of spiritlessness, for Kierkegaard – 'corrupt most people, so that they become thoughtless.'[20] At first sight this looks just like Kant's negative view of habit in the moral sphere, transposed to a religious context. 'I hate habitual Christianity in whatever form it appears,' wrote Kierkegaard in 1851, adding that this 'can indeed have many forms', ranging from bourgeois complacency to 'the kind of habitual Christianity which is found in the sects, the enthusiasts, the super-orthodox.'[21] Although Kant and Kierkegaard disagree about what the good life involves, they both argue that habit breeds thoughtlessness and undermines our freedom.

However, Kierkegaard's perspective on the question of habit is very different from Kant's, for his philosophy is oriented to a specific historical situation: the decline of Christian faith. 'Times are different, and have different requirements,' he wrote in his journal in 1850: here he envisages Luther returning in the 'indolent' nineteenth century, and demanding that 'works should be accentuated again.'[22] This reminds us that Kierkegaard's critique of habit is itself (in part, at least) a symptom of historical circumstance. If he were to return to Copenhagen in the secular, individualistic twenty-first century, perhaps he would argue that custom should be accentuated again. Kierkegaard's polemic against habitual religion seems less pertinent now that the decline of Christian faith has advanced so much further. Going to church on a Sunday might now seem countercultural, for in many parts of modern Europe religious practice often swims against the current of secular orthodoxy, and has even become a form of dissent.

In Kierkegaard's own time, Lutheran Christianity – which once represented a radical alternative to the established church – was institutionalized in the Danish state church, and fully absorbed into the customs and culture of Denmark. Kierkegaard associates the idea that Christian faith has become a 'second nature' with a spiritual complacency that obscures the real meaning of religious life. In 1843 the theologian Hans Lassen Martensen, an influential advocate of Hegelian ideas in Copenhagen, claimed that in the modern period, 'when the Church had put out its firm roots in the world, God's kingdom had become just like nature.'[23] Similarly, Kierkegaard suggests that centuries of Christian practice have resulted in the 'naturalisation and domestication' of an originally scandalous, countercultural teaching. 'Over eighteen centuries,' he writes, 'Christianity has permeated all relations of life, reshaped the world.' Unlike Martensen, though, he regards this as a process of decline rather than progression, for it produces 'an illusion by which the resolving and choosing subject is trapped.'[24]

It is often pointed out that one of the great benefits of habit is to make life easier – and this is why Ravaisson describes habit as a 'law of grace' that facilitates the good life. According to Kierkegaard, however, custom has made faith *too easy*, as if one became a Christian simply by being baptized, learning a catechism, and going to church on Sundays. In becoming habitual, he suggests, Christianity has declined into 'a secular-minded thoughtlessness that nonchalantly goes on living in the illusion of being Christian.'[25] Arguing that this complacency obscures the infinitely demanding character of religious faith, he sets himself the peculiar task of 'making Christianity more difficult.'[26]

Kierkegaard's strategy in recovering the meaning of faith from the degrading effects of habit and custom has a theoretical and a practical dimension: he wants to show that faith is both difficult (if not impossible) to understand, and difficult (if not impossible) to accomplish. In place of the secure familiarity of habitual religion, Kierkegaard offers anxiety and paradox, fear and trembling. Using 'indirect' methods inspired by Socratic philosophy, he seeks to show his readers that they neither understand nor possess Christian faith – just as Socrates questioned his fellow Athenians to show them that they neither understood nor possessed virtue. For both philosophers, these methods aim to demonstrate that genuine virtue, or faith, is not reducible to conventional practices, beliefs and values. Opening up this gap between custom and an authentic conception of the good life both makes this conception something inherently *questionable*, and creates room for the pursuit of wisdom, or the task of becoming a Christian.

Although Socrates and Kierkegaard are disruptive and anti-conformist thinkers, they also recognize that virtue, or faith, must be lived in the world, with other people, and therefore demands engagement in the very forms of life that fall short of their (often elusive) ideals. This means that authentic existence is always ironic: it participates in the conventional world in a way that expresses an aspiration for truth or meaning that is not contained by that world.[27] Kierkegaard's ironic question, 'In Christendom, is there a single Christian?' suggests that Christianity is a task that cannot be circumscribed by the customs and practices which constitute a Christian culture. But this question is simultaneously a call to authentically inhabit these particular customs and practices: to become a Christian within Christendom, not elsewhere. Indeed, Christian faith involves commitment to the church community – however unsatisfactory this may be in its quotidian reality – and belief in the efficacy of the sacrament of communion. One solution that Kierkegaard himself found to this dilemma was to attend communion on Fridays, instead of on Sundays. This seemed to provide a way of participating in the Christian community without thereby falling into a pseudo-spiritual routine – although this was only possible for Kierkegaard because he had received a large inheritance from his father, and did not have to work during the week. He wrote several sermon-like discourses for the occasion of Friday communion, and in these he emphasizes that one should be drawn to church by 'heartfelt longing', and not by force of 'habit or common practice'.[28]

While he insists that habitual repetition undermines authentic faith, Kierkegaard places a different kind of repetition at the heart of the Christian life. Indeed, this new concept of repetition is informed by his Lutheran view that grace cannot be possessed in the form of a *habitus*. If human sinfulness is a tendency to refuse God – a Lockean disposition that, like a coiled spring, is 'ready upon every occasion to break into action', and so continually reasserts itself – then, Kierkegaard argues, divine grace cannot take root within us. In one of his *Four Upbuilding Discourses* (1843) on the theme of the gift, he develops the idea that grace must be repeatedly given again, 'as a blessing that the soul is constantly losing.'[29] Reflecting on one of his favourite biblical texts, 'Every good and every perfect gift is from above' (James 1:17), he argues that we do not even possess the capacity to receive the divine gift: 'God is the only one who gives in such a way that he gives the condition [for receiving it] along with the gift, the only one who in giving has already given. God gives both [the power] to will and to bring to completion; he begins and completes the good work in a person.'[30] Furthermore, he claims that 'the need [for God] itself is a good and a perfect gift from God.'[31]

For Kierkegaard, the very concept of gift is based on loss rather than possession: 'the gift [does not] belong to the needy one as a possession, *because he has received it as a gift*.'[32] And this means that repetition is integral to his logic of the gift: grace has to renew itself continually because it is repeatedly lost. Our tendency to refuse God means that the restoration of our relationship with God – which is the content of the gift – needs to be 'offered anew in each moment.'[33] But Kierkegaard also suggests that the movement of faith involves giving up our gifts, precisely so that we can receive them back again in a new way. This is why he thinks that Abraham, who sacrifices Isaac in order to 'receive a son a second time, contrary to expectation', is the highest exemplar of religious faith.[34] Both aspects of the loss of the gift – loss through sin, and loss through faith – involve repetition, and both are expressions of human freedom. For Kierkegaard, the continuous oscillation between gift and loss is the elemental rhythm of existence, the pulse of the spiritual life as it flows between immanence and transcendence, just as Deleuze's 'tick-tock' or heartbeat exemplifies the basic repetition from which natural life takes shape. This oscillation between losing and gaining, giving up and receiving back again, constitutes the form of our temporality, the undulating pathway of human freedom in the world.

Kierkegaard's concept of non-habitual repetition articulates a theology of grace that is clearly indebted to Luther. However, he also provides a more philosophical account of this concept. In *Repetition* (1843) he suggests that the difference between habitual and free repetition rests on the distinction between actuality and possibility. Habits develop when something actual is repeated – a particular action or experience, a gesture or a phrase. But repetition of a possibility constitutes human freedom. For Kierkegaard, possibility is not just a modal category, but an existential fact: it signifies the moment of decision. Once a choice has been made, a possibility actualized, the situation may develop in two ways: either the chosen action can be repeated, or the choice itself can be taken again. The outward appearance might be the same in each case. You might, for example, buy a coffee on Monday morning and on Tuesday morning, and then on Wednesday morning either habitually buy a coffee, or make a choice and again decide on coffee. In this instance, the difference between the two kinds of repetition seems inconsequential. But when the possibility in question is something like being married, or being a Christian, then *how* you repeat yourself becomes extremely significant: a matter of freedom or bondage, of spiritual life or death. One way of repeating, suggests Kierkegaard, leads to the degradation of habit and custom; the other way renews freedom, and thus preserves it. It is this free relation to her existence that enables a person to live in fidelity to herself through time.

This theory finds an application in the practice of baptizing young children, which is a difficult issue for Kierkegaard. On the one hand, he acknowledges the importance of belonging to the Christian community; on the other hand, he insists that this belonging should not be reduced to customary rituals. In *Concluding Unscientific Postscript* he articulates the idea that spiritual repetition concerns the possible, not the actual, by suggesting that those born into a Christian culture, who undergo the 'custom' of infant baptism, must 'transform [this] initial being-Christian into a possibility in order to become Christian in truth.'[35] Similarly, in *The Concept of Anxiety* (1844) he writes of the 'originality in earnestness' that makes repetition free: 'When the originality in earnestness is acquired and preserved, then there is succession and repetition; as soon as originality is lacking in repetition there is habit. The earnest person is earnest precisely through the originality with which he returns in repetition.'[36] This thought is crystallized in Kierkegaard's journal:

> Earnestness is acquired originality.
> Different from habit — which is the disappearance of self-awareness.
> Therefore genuine repetition is — earnestness.[37]

To illustrate his point, Kierkegaard envisages a clergyman who every Sunday recites the common prayer and baptizes several children. What is required of this man is not 'feeling' or 'enthusiasm', which have variable effects, but earnestness, which is 'alone capable of returning every Sunday with the same originality to the same thing . . . This same thing to which earnestness is to return is earnestness itself . . . Inwardness, certitude, is earnestness.'[38]

Kierkegaard's analysis of repetition draws out a new aspect of the ambiguous relationship between habit and freedom. He emphasizes that freedom is essential to the human condition: whether we like it or not, we are haunted by possibility – by the awareness that things might have been otherwise, and could still be otherwise if we choose differently. This freedom, he argues, always makes us anxious, as if possibility were an abyss we might fall into at any moment. 'Anxiety is freedom's actuality as the possibility of possibility,' he writes.[39] If Maine de Biran discovered that effort is the physical feeling of resistance, Kierkegaard discovered that anxiety is the spiritual feeling of freedom. And habit, of course, is a way of dealing with this feeling. The comfort of familiarity and routine soothes the nervous system; it takes the edge off anxiety by drawing us back from the edge of possibility. But does this mean that habit is a symptom of freedom's anxiety, or a remedy for it? Kierkegaard certainly thinks that habit is pathological rather than therapeutic – and this insight would be developed by Freud, who found that the compulsion to repeat is a common symptom of neurosis. From a Kierkegaardian perspective, habit is an anxious attempt to repress freedom, to evade ethical and spiritual responsibility. Instead of diverting our anxiety or seeking relief, he suggests, we should 'learn to be anxious in the right way': to feel our freedom, and to regard it as both a gift and a task that directs our attention to God.[40]

RECEPTIVITY AND RESISTANCE

In response to the Protestant Reformation, the Roman Catholic Church reaffirmed the doctrine that God's grace can be possessed by Christians in the form of a *habitus*. Since the Council of Trent, the distinction between 'actual' and 'habitual' grace has been part of official Catholic teaching. These English terms are misleading if they imply that habitual grace is something more mundane and less real than actual grace: in fact, the contrast is between direct action by God in the world, and the gift of a *habitus* that puts the power to do good in human hands. But although the word 'habitual' may not convey to an ordinary person the philosophical concept of *habitus*, this translation points to an interesting connection between the Catholic doctrine of grace and a more familiar idea of habit as involving repetition, custom and practice.

This connection becomes explicit in the sacrament of the Eucharist, an essential part of Christian life for Catholics and Protestants alike. The Eucharist is one of our culture's long-standing habits: it has been practised as a Christian ritual daily, repeatedly, and in diverse circumstances for two thousand years – and of course its roots in the Jewish Passover meal stretch far further back. Indeed, it is a ceremonious, ritualized form of the very ancient human habit of gathering together for a meal. This seems to be a fundamental expression of a communal *hexis*, and like any *hexis* it is essentially temporal. The habit of sharing food and drink both embodies a cultural heritage and provides sustenance for continuing life, so that through this repetition a family or community holds itself together in relation to its past and its future. And, since gathering for a meal involves sharing a certain time and space, this custom is always localized and particular – and yet it also instantiates a universal form of human interaction. In taking up and spiritualizing all these elements, the eucharistic ritual embodies and reflects back to us a constituent of our cultural life, at once simple and profound, that we may be inclined to take for granted. It should not be surprising, then, that reflection on this particular religious practice can illuminate the nature of practice itself.

The Eucharist is a complex ritual that commemorates the Last Supper, makes an offering to God on behalf of the Christian community, and – somehow – communicates grace and forgiveness to those who consume the consecrated bread and wine. How this works is a matter of intense theological debate. But one way or another, the Eucharist is concerned with the repetition of grace. In the liturgy of the Mass the idea of being changed by repetition is made explicit. And the consumption of bread and wine physically enacts the process of appropriation that characterizes habit and practice. This signifies that grace is renewed or replenished, and at the same time becomes more deeply embedded, more natural. In the Eucharist, then, the ontologically slippery concept of a disposition finds a visible, albeit mysterious, expression. Whether the sacrament effects or simply performs a gift of divine grace is, of course, a question of faith. However, the simple phenomenon of habit indicates that we are altered by repetition, so that even without the help of faith we can make some sense of the idea that genuine change takes place in a religious ritual. We have seen that the principle of habit involves plasticity, self-modification, *auto-poesis*: because our natures are receptive to change, we gradually form and re-form ourselves through our own actions and experiences. When we put to one side the supernatural dimension of grace, and focus on what is performed humanly in this practice, we see a dramatization of practice as such.

Taking communion involves a posture of receptivity: the recipient holds out her hands to accept what the priest offers her, bowing her head in thanks, and consumes the sacrament. This posture embodies the theological idea that 'her' virtue, while genuinely hers, has its source in God. When the ritual is repeated regularly, it serves as a reminder that helps to maintain, in the lives of believers, the connection between freedom and dependence that is so central to Christian doctrine. More generally, the sacrament of the Eucharist is for Christians the ultimate expression of receptivity to God, the highest good. But it is a gesture of resistance as well as receptivity. It enacts a turning-away from more worldly or aesthetic activities: a lazy Sunday morning, the weekend papers, a game of tennis, *The Archers* omnibus, for example. More inwardly, too, the whole process of taking communion – including the prayers that precede and follow it – involves a certain dynamic of receptivity and resistance. Since the practice will be most meaningful when it is enacted attentively, not mechanically, participants should resist the pull of distracting thoughts and try to remain present to the experience of the sacrament. This particular dynamic of receptivity and resistance combines openness and discipline: a simple openness to whatever benefits the practice may bring, and a disciplined effort to be attentive.

Receptivity and resistance are, we have seen, the twin conditions of habit. Any being that is able to acquire a habit – to be formed by events, and to maintain a stable form over time – must be both receptive and resistant to change. In the Eucharist these fundamental conditions come into view, are performed, and express a specific ethical-religious meaning.

This provides a clue to an important aspect of habit, and helps to further clarify the distinction between ordinary habit and practice. In all kinds of habit acquisition we modify our manner of receptivity and resistance; we become more or less receptive to certain influences, and more or less resistant to others. We create a particular pattern of receiving and resisting that comes to characterize our whole way of being in the world. In ordinary habit this happens unconsciously. In practice, however, this modification is oriented to an idea of the good, to an explicitly desired goal − whether this is becoming a piano player, an athlete, or a virtuous person. And in certain kinds of practice, receptivity and resistance are themselves made explicit. If ordinary practice is an elevation of habit that takes repetition as a method and a goal, ethical or spiritual practice elevates this ordinary form of practice by aiming to develop receptivity to the good, and resistance to whatever hinders or threatens this.

Although the Eucharist dramatizes this structure of practice in a distinctive way, it is not the only practice that has such a structure. The more inward qualities of this ritual − openness and discipline, attentiveness and commitment, a fine balance of activity and passivity − are essential elements of contemplative practices such as prayer and meditation. These are at the heart of all religious traditions: they are usually a source of inspiration and teaching, and are developed intensively in monastic and ascetic forms of life. Spiritual practices employ a wide range of techniques to increase receptivity to the good, whether this is conceived as God or as the practitioner's own true nature. Such techniques include repetition of words or mantras; attention to the breath, to bodily sensations, or to one's inner being; or simply silence and stillness, within which insight naturally arises. Like the

Eucharist, they also require resistance to distraction and temptation. And they usually involve a certain posture of the body, a gesture of the hands, which quietly expresses the inner quality of the practice. In Patanjali's handbook of spiritual practice, the *Yoga Sutras*, the twin principles of receptivity and resistance to change (or movement) are at the heart of the bodily postures (*asanas*) that help to lead the mind towards union with God. In his chapter on practice (*sadhana*) Patanjali states that yoga postures should be at once steady, firm, strong (*sthira*) and comfortable, relaxed, open (*sukham*), thus indicating in a single verse a middle way between rigidity and formlessness: *sthira sukham asanam.*[41]

This brings us to our image of the pathway, and to the idea of a spiritual path. What it means to follow such a path may be illuminated further by reflection on one of our oldest habits of all: walking, 'the human way of getting about'.[42] Normally, lost in thought, we pay little attention to the thoughtless wisdom of the body which knows how to walk around things, under things, over things, uphill, down stairs, through sand and snow and water. We rarely notice, for example, the quiet movements of our muscles and joints; our receptivity and resistance to the force of gravity; the sway of the hips back and forth, side to side; the marvellous cooperation between the left leg and the right; air passing across our face and hands; the undulations of the whole body as our feet rise and fall. Like eating, walking can be a practice as well as a habit. This elevation of the mundane may happen not only in the context of pilgrimage, but in a daily meditative exercise that takes us, along the path of attentiveness, from a familiar activity to an experience at once mysterious and revelatory, poetic and down to earth. A way of walking can disclose a way of being in the world – a habitual manner of carrying oneself inwardly as well as outwardly.[43]

The distinctive qualities of religious practice suggest a definition of the good life as the intelligent cultivation of a pattern of receptivity and resistance. Habit (in the sense of *consuetudo*) and practice are part of the process of cultivation, but the pattern that is thereby formed is itself a habit (in the sense of *habitus*): a disposition or 'way of being' that is – like walking – at once stable and dynamic, consistent and responsive. This is rather different from the account of moral education outlined by William James, who certainly grasps both the power of repetition and the importance of attentiveness:

> The hell to be endured hereafter, of which theology tells, is no worse than the hell we make for ourselves in this world by habitually fashioning our characters in the wrong way. Could the young but realise how soon they will become mere walking bundles of habit, they would give more heed to their conduct while in the plastic state. We are spinning our own fates, good or evil, and never to be undone. Every smallest stroke of virtue or of vice leaves its never so little scar . . . Young people should know this truth in advance.[44]

Here, James suggests that plasticity is a feature of youth, implying that as we grow older we become increasingly rigid and mechanical: 'in most of us, by the age of thirty, the character has set like plaster, and will never soften again.'[45] This may well be the usual way of things, but, as we have seen, human habit need not be the ossification of nature, but rather its modification, even its spiritualization. Even if it is true

135 **Habit, faith and grace**

that old dogs cannot learn new tricks, old people can certainly remain receptive to new ideas, new experiences, new capacities.

If receptivity and resistance are the conditions of life as well as of habit, then the good life consists in, first, preserving these conditions and, second, orienting them in the right way. And on a practical level, acquiring wisdom and virtue means not only learning *what* is good, but also learning how to be receptive to it. As we have seen, this involves resistance. It is only through living that we come to know how different experiences and activities – and, in particular, different people – affect us. Even those ethical doctrines that emphasize a radical openness to others (loving one's enemies, turning the other cheek, being unconditionally hospitable to all) must also teach resistance to negative influence, which requires discriminating judgment. After all, most of the purest spiritual teachings require practitioners to swim against the stream, to resist the path of least resistance.

We have seen that there are different conceptions of the good life, and that aesthetic, ethical and religious perspectives provide different criteria of existential value. The various approaches to living well within these alternative spheres all involve cultivating a certain pattern of receptivity and resistance. But the aesthetic sphere does not require an objective notion of the good to orient our way of being: here, living well means being receptive to pleasurable experiences and resistant to unpleasant ones. Since the subjective effects of encounters and experiences change over time, the best pattern of receptivity and resistance may be one that is itself continually in flux. On the other hand, an ethical-religious conception of an objective value or *telos* will anchor a stable pattern of receptivity and resistance. Of course, this should not be static or rigid: different situations invite different responses, and there are many ways of expressing an orientation to the good. This distinction between the aesthetic and ethical-religious perspectives mirrors the contrast between pragmatic and truth-oriented accounts of the relationship between habit and knowledge, which we considered in Chapter 2.

The difficulty, of course, is that even if we believe in the reality of truth and goodness, they are seldom easy to discern. By the time we begin a serious search for them we are often already in the middle of our lives, with a history of painful mistakes which, as William James puts it, have left their scars and cannot be undone. Spinoza acknowledges that 'all human beings are born in a state of complete ignorance, and before they can learn the true way of life and acquire a virtuous disposition, even if they have been well brought up, a great part of their life has gone by.'[46] And this, it seems, is the best we can hope for. If we happen to grow up in a culture that pretends to instantiate wisdom and virtue, but in fact obscures these qualities and promotes their opposite, then we will be trained, before we know any better, in a pattern of receptivity and resistance that needs to be unravelled before any real progress can be made. At first, we will discover only that we are established in a way of life that has rendered us insensitive to the good, and inclines us in the wrong direction. Collective, cultural delusions can be so entrenched, self-perpetuating, and all-encompassing that it takes the disruptive genius of a Socrates or a Kierkegaard to penetrate them. If being human enables us to elevate habit into practice, and even to elevate practice into enlightenment, it also makes us vulnerable to a world of confusing, ambiguous, and endlessly complex influences. This is why, as Spinoza admits at the end of his *Ethics*, living a genuinely good life is 'as difficult as it is rare'.[47]

NOTES

1 Augustine, *The City of God against the Pagans*, trans. R. W. Dyson (Cambridge: Cambridge University Press, 1998), p. 919.

2 Augustine, *Confessions*, trans. Henry Chadwick (London: Penguin, 1961), p. 164. On habit in Augustine, see John Prendiville, 'The Development of the Idea of Habit in the Thought of St. Augustine', *Traditio* 28 (1972): 29–99.

3 Ibid., p. 165.

4 Félix Ravaisson, *Of Habit*, trans. Clare Carlisle and Mark Sinclair (London: Continuum, 2008), p. 57.

5 Thomas Aquinas, *Summa theologiae*, vol. 23: *Virtue (Ia2ae 55–67)*, trans. W. D. Hughes (Oxford: Blackfriars; and London: Eyre & Spottiswoode, 1969), p. 11 (I-II.55.4)

6 Thomas Aquinas, *Disputed Questions on Virtue*, trans. E. M. Watkins (Cambridge: Cambridge University Press, 2005), p. 8 (art. 1, *My reply*).

7 Martin Luther, *Letters I*, ed. and trans. Gottfried G. Krodel, vol. 48 of *Luther's Works* (Philadelphia: Fortress Press, 1963), p. 25. On Luther's critique of *habitus*, see B. Lohse, *Martin Luther's Theology: Its Historical and Systematic Development*, trans. Roy A. Harrisville (Minneapolis: Fortress Press, 2006), pp. 47–50, 59–60, 72, 261; G. Ebeling, *Luther*, trans. R. A. Wilson (London: Collins, 1970), pp. 70–71.

8 Martin Luther, *Lectures on Romans*, ed. Hilton C. Oswald, vol. 25 of *Luther's Works* (St Louis: Concordia, 1972), pp. 251–52.

9 Ibid., p. 257. See Lohse, *Martin Luther's Theology*, p. 73; Ebeling, *Luther*, p. 71; Heiko Oberman, *The Dawn of the Reformation* (Edinburgh: T. & T. Clark, 1986), p. 121.

10 Ibid., p. 227.

11 Ibid., p. 136.

12 Ravaisson, *Of Habit*, p. 69.

13 See Ravaisson, *Of Habit*, p. 55: 'In reflection and will, the end of movement is an idea, an ideal to be accomplished . . . It is a possibility to be realised. But as the end becomes fused with the movement, and the movement with the tendency, possibility, the ideal is realised in it. The *idea* becomes *being*, the very being of the movement and of the tendency determined by the idea. Habit becomes more and more a substantial idea.' Ravaisson writes here of 'possibility' rather than 'potentiality', which, as he indicates with his reference to 'reflection and will', suggests an account of what is going on in the exercise of a disposition that is more voluntarist and intellectualist than the account

I am outlining here. Historically, this can probably be explained by the fact that on this point Ravaisson takes his lead from Leibniz rather than Aquinas.

14 See Simon Oliver, 'The Sweet Delight of Virtue and Grace in Aquinas's Ethics', *International Journal of Systematic Theology* 7, no. 1 (2005): 52–71.

15 Ravaisson, *Of Habit*, p. 69.

16 Aquinas, *Disputed Questions on Virtue*, p. 10 (art. 1, *Replies to Objections*).

17 *Hegel's Philosophy of Right*, trans. T. M. Knox (Oxford: Oxford University Press, 1952), p. 260.

18 Søren Kierkegaard, *Concluding Unscientific Postscript*, vol. 1, trans. Edna H. Hong and Howard V. Hong (Princeton: Princeton University Press, 1992), p. 340.

19 Ibid., p. 364.

20 Ibid., p. 47.

21 Søren Kierkegaard, 'An Open Letter to Dr. Rudelbach', in *The Corsair Affair*, trans. Howard V. Hong and Edna H. Hong (Princeton: Princeton University Press, 2009), p. 52.

22 *Søren Kierkegaards Papirer*, 16 vols, 2nd edn, ed. P. A. Heiberg, V. Kuhr, E. Torsting, and N. Thulstrup (Copenhagen: Gyldendal, 1968–78),X B 2 (1851).

23 Martensen, *The Christian Faith*, cited in S. Kierkegaard, *Philosophical Fragments*, trans. Howard V. Hong and Edna H. Hong (Princeton: Princeton University Press, 1985), p. 316.

24 Kierkegaard, *Concluding Unscientific Postscript*, p. 585.

25 Kierkegaard, 'Open Letter to Dr. Rudelbach', p. 52.

26 Kierkegaard, *Concluding Unscientific Postscript*, pp. 241, 383–84.

27 See Jonathan Lear, *A Case for Irony* (Cambridge, MA: Harvard University Press, 2011); George Pattison, *Kierkegaard and the Theology of the Nineteenth Century* (Oxford: Oxford University Press, 2012), pp. 211–13.

28 Søren Kierkegaard, *Discourses at the Communion on Fridays*, trans. Sylvia Walsh (Bloomington: Indiana University Press, 2011), p. 39.

29 Søren Kierkegaard, 'Every Good and Every Perfect Gift Is from Above', in *Eighteen Upbuilding Discourses*, trans. Howard V. Hong and Edna H. Hong (Princeton: Princeton University Press, 1992), p. 127.

30 Ibid., p. 134.

31 Ibid., p. 139.

32 Ibid., p. 157 (my emphasis).

33 Ibid., p. 126.

34 Søren Kierkegaard, *Fear and Trembling*, trans. Howard V. Hong and Edna H. Hong (Princeton: Princeton University Press, 1983), p. 9.

35 Kierkegaard, *Concluding Unscientific Postscript*, p. 365.

36 Søren Kierkegaard, *The Concept of Anxiety*, trans. Reidar Thomte (Princeton: Princeton University Press, 1981), p. 149.

37 Ibid., p. 327.

38 Ibid., pp. 149–51.

39 Ibid., p. 42.

40 Ibid., p. 154.

41 Patanjali, *Yoga Sutras*, ch. 2, v. 46.

42 Thomas A. Clark, *In Praise of Walking* (Pittenweem: Moschatel Press, 2004).

43 Meditation on walking may simply yield the insight 'I am walking', but it has also inspired an extensive poetic literature: see the Buddha's teaching in the *Mahasatipatthana Sutta* (*Iriyapathapabbam*); Rebecca Solnit, *Wanderlust: A History of Walking* (London: Verso, 2001); Tim Ingold and Jo Lee Vergunst (eds), *Ways of Walking* (Aldershot: Ashgate, 2008); Robert Macfarlane, *The Old Ways*, esp. ch. 2.

44 William James, *Psychology: Briefer Course* (Cambridge, MA: Harvard University Press, 1984), p. 138.

45 Ibid., p. 133.

46 Spinoza, *Tractatus Theologico-Politicus*, trans. Samuel Shirley (Leiden: E. J. Brill, 1989), p. 238 (ch. 16).

47 Spinoza, *Ethics*, trans. Edwin Curley, E5P42, scholium.

Conclusion

Activities that go under the name of philosophy perennially invite critique, just as virtue continues to call for Socratic or Kierkegaardian irony. Our attempts to do philosophy tend to fall far short of the ancient Greek ideal of love of truth and goodness. While we aspire to wisdom, we often end up with cliché and unwitting self-parody – like the public speaker envisaged by Bergson, whose intelligence is betrayed by his mechanical gestures. What is laughable in this case, though, is the foolish complacency of cleverness. Each philosophical method offers a potential path of least resistance, a rut to get stuck in, a bandwagon to jump on – in sum, a minefield of mindlessness. Sometimes there is a fine line between rigour and rigor mortis. But our methods are also ways of keeping thought alive by overcoming, subverting or penetrating habit. There is an intimate connection between habit and philosophical method, and therefore this too displays the ambivalence that has been traced in the preceding chapters.

There are many philosophical methods, but making distinctions is one of the most basic and ubiquitous tools of philosophy. A series of distinctions have structured our analysis of habit: receptivity and resistance; *ethos* and *hexis*; *consuetudo* and *habitus*; capacity and tendency; active habit and passive habituation; animal and human habit; physical and psychological habit; individual habit and collective custom; habit and practice. We have seen that habit cuts across and unsettles distinctions between permanence and change, mind and body, freedom and necessity, life and death. And all these distinctions play a part in illuminating the ambiguity and ambivalence that seem to follow habit wherever it goes.

We have seen that the 'double law of habit' is an important philosophical discovery, and this law operates on philosophy as on other activities. Philosophy is a discipline that is cultivated with effort, rather than an ordinary habit we fall into. Thinking always involves a combination of activity and passivity, but philosophical thinking should be more active than passive. Learning to philosophize means becoming more discriminating about concepts, language and arguments, and less subject to the images and associations that flow unbidden through our minds. This means that the double law of habit should influence the philosopher as it influences the discerning wine expert, and not as it affects the casual drinker. The philosopher becomes a connoisseur of concepts: her intellectual perceptions are refined as her resistance to clear, sustained thought declines.

On the basis of our reflection on habit, we can understand philosophical method as a set of techniques to transform the passivity of ordinary thinking into an active practice. These techniques include systematic doubt, such as that practised by Descartes in his *Meditations*; phenomenology, which brackets the question of objective reality and provides detailed descriptions of the content of consciousness; critique (feminist critique, Marxist critique, psychoanalytic critique, for example); and deconstruction, the method of reading pioneered by Derrida that focuses on the marginal, unwritten and self-subverting aspects of a text. In using such methods the philosopher seeks to refresh intellectual perception, as an artist refreshes sensual perception. Just as art can re-present everyday experience as remarkable and beautiful (think of the interior scenes painted by Vermeer or Hopper, or the landscapes of Van Gogh or Monet), so philosophical method often involves stating the obvious, so that the things we take for granted can be attended to. Alternatively, philosophers use imaginative thought experiments to render uncanny what is most familiar to us. One of the best examples of this strategy is in Condillac's *Treatise on Sensations*, where a statue is given, one by one, powers of sensing and movement. 'We must put ourselves in [the statue's] place,' writes Condillac, 'and deprive ourselves entirely of all our habits.'[1] He suggests that readers who do this will have 'no difficulty' in understanding his treatise, whereas those who do not will encounter 'enormous difficulties'. The source of these difficulties is habit, which 'does not allow us to perceive the sequence of our judgements.'[2]

Because language is deeply habitual – learned by imitation and repetition, and entrenched by common usage – it often becomes a transparent, inconspicuous medium that simultaneously carries and conceals meaning. Nietzsche argues, provocatively as usual, that truth is merely 'a moveable host of metaphors . . . which, after long usage, seem to a people to be canonical, fixed and binding.' Custom and convention, he suggests, make us forget that these 'truths' are illusions: they are 'worn out' metaphors that have been 'drained of sensuous force'.[3] It is not surprising that many philosophers try to recover meaning by unsettling entrenched linguistic habits. Nietzsche, who was trained in philology, uses genealogical analysis of words and concepts as a powerful critical technique. Heidegger both excavates old, concealed meanings and forms strange neologisms; in particular, he turns nouns into verbs – 'the world worlds' – to unsettle the habit of conceptualizing existences as things, objects, substances. Michel Foucault, on the other hand, applies Nietzsche's genealogical method to the practices and institutions in which concepts are embedded.[4] More cautious methods of linguistic analysis, such as Wittgenstein's intense reflection on everyday forms of expression, are less historically oriented, but nevertheless aim to penetrate the veil of habit. The use of symbolic logic strips away language altogether, in order to distil pure reason from the obfuscating clamour of worn-out metaphors. At the other end of this spectrum, poetic philosophical writing draws attention to the materiality of language, thickening what has become transparent and inconspicuous.

If philosophers need a method to sustain the activity of thinking and to disclose the familiar, they also need habit to facilitate their work. We have already seen that Descartes and Spinoza, like the Stoics before them, advocate practices of intellectual discipline and attentiveness even as they battle against habitual ways of thinking. In a similar vein, Hegel notes that studying formal logic promotes 'the habit of attending to our inward selves'.[5] More prosaically, perhaps – but no less importantly – habit can, by its influence on passivity, overcome physical and psychological resistance to intellectual effort. Hegel reminds us that even when our thinking becomes 'pure and active' it has a corporeal dimension, and thus 'requires habit and familiarity'. 'Want of habit and too-long-continued thinking cause headache,' he adds, but 'habit diminishes this feeling.'[6] Hegel's own writing must have caused hundreds of headaches over the years, but his most committed readers will testify that even *The Science of Logic* can be read painlessly with the help of habit. But if habit facilitates thinking, it may also bring it to an end. Peirce suggests that habit brings a kind of intellectual comfort, just as it promotes physical ease – and he implies here that habit replaces active thought: 'it appeases the irritation of doubt, which is the motive for thinking, thought relaxes, and comes to rest for a moment when belief is reached.'[7]

Other habits, and especially daily routines, support philosophical work less directly. This takes us back to William James's observation that the 'effortless custody of automatism' liberates our 'higher powers of mind' – but habit does not merely take care of mundane practical matters, nor accomplish only the more physical aspects of our work, such as writing or typing. Certain habits can become, more positively, generative of thought: walking, smoking, or drinking coffee, for example. Kierkegaard liked to do all three: he was a familiar figure on the streets of Copenhagen, and his idiosyncratic habit made him easily recognizable, for he was a little lopsided and, finding it difficult to walk in a straight line, zigzagged across the pavement. At home, he worked standing at a high writing desk so that he could walk about the room as he composed aloud his elaborate sentences. Kant, too, was a notorious walker: his afternoon perambulations in Königsberg were, it is said, as regular as clockwork. Other thinkers – Descartes and Proust, for example – have found lying in bed to be more conducive to intellectual work.

How does the double law of habit influence the existential kind of philosophy that takes seriously Socrates's injunction 'Know thyself'? Just as Hume points out that custom 'not only covers our natural ignorance, but even conceals itself,' so Kierkegaard writes that habit 'is cunning enough never to let itself be seen.' 'Habit is not like other enemies that one sees and against which one aggressively defends oneself,' he continues, for 'the struggle is actually with oneself in getting to see it.' If habits 'constitute the self' – if 'we are habits, nothing but habits' – then the struggle to gain sight of habit is the task of Socratic philosophy.[8] Although this sort of assertion may be excessive, it is still clear that habit shapes our identity in all sorts of profound and subtle ways. Our habits are myriad ways of carrying ourselves through the world; ways of holding our selves in being. But when we seek self-knowledge, we are trying to reflect on ourselves not simply as objects, but as subjects: we are attempting to see *how we see*, to think about *how we think*. And if our ways of seeing and thinking are themselves conditioned by habit, how can we ever complete the task of self-investigation? Are we hopelessly chasing our own tails when we try to know ourselves? Will habit always remain a blind spot in the examined life – a blind spot which can move, change shape and contract, but never disappears? And is this blind spot, in fact, essential to every life?

Some philosophies of habit seem to suggest just this: Proust writes that 'if habit is a second nature, it prevents us from knowing our first.' And this view receives support and explanation in Maine de Biran's analysis of self-consciousness. In discussing the influence of habit on our thinking, Maine de Biran argues that we become aware of ourselves through the effort we must make when we encounter any kind of resistance: that we feel *ourselves* making a difficult movement, or that we feel *ourselves* thinking a difficult thought. However, 'the most common effect of habit is to take away all resistance, to destroy all friction.'[9] When habit makes our movements and thoughts easier, we not only notice these less, but also become less self-aware: 'this *me* [*moi*], which escapes itself in the apparent simplicity and extreme facility of its own acts, which ceaselessly eludes itself and is everywhere present to itself . . . how should one *reflect* on its habits, the most intimate, the most profound of all?'[10] This application of the double law of habit has the apparently paradoxical consequence that our consciousness of ourselves diminishes as we become more adept at thinking.

If it is possible to see our habits, and thus to see ourselves more clearly, then the kind of seeing that is required here is not rational reflection, which, so to speak, attempts to look down at habit from above. Much more effective will be an attentiveness to thoughts, physical sensations and emotional responses that catches habit in the act. Similarly, once habits come into view they will not easily be broken by an act of choice. This means that self-knowledge involves both more and less than the light of reason and the force of will. It involves a discerning familiarity with habit itself, which learns when a habit should be broken, and when it is good to surrender to the deliverance of earlier effort. Patience is an essential virtue in cultivating this wisdom, for patience is the ability to deal excellently with tenacity, with tendencies, with repetition – it is habit's own virtue. As awareness seeps into our habits it gradually transforms them. Kierkegaard tells us that 'the person who sees the habit is saved from the habit.'[11] At other times, of course, seeing a habit allows us to be thankful for it, instead of taking its grace for granted. Either way, when philosophy takes this path of patient, disciplined attentiveness it ceases to be merely a clever synthesis of clichés. It becomes less and less an ordinary habit, more and more a contemplative practice that, knowing by acquaintance, turns the soul slowly towards wisdom. When we feel heavy-laden by iron chains of habit, we may at least trust that the movement will, through repetition, get easier.

NOTES

1 Étienne Bonnot de Condillac, *Treatise on Sensations*, trans. M. G. Carr (London: Favil Press, 1930), p. 57.

2 Ibid., pp. 69–70 and preface.

3 Friedrich Nietzsche, 'On Truth and Lies in a Nonmoral Sense', in *Philosophy and Truth: Selections from Nietzsche's Notebooks of the Early 1870s*, trans. and ed. Daniel Breazeale (Atlantic Highlands, NJ: Humanities Press, 1999), p. 84.

4 See Johanna Oksala, 'The Neo-Liberal Subject of Feminism: From Discipline to Self-Advancement', *Journal of the British Society for Phenomenology* 42, no. 1 (2011), pp. 104–20.

5 *Hegel's Logic: Being Part One of the Encyclopaedia of the Philosophical Sciences* (1830), trans. William Wallace (Oxford: Clarendon Press, 1975), §20, *Zuzatz*.

6 *Hegel's Philosophy of Mind* (Part Three of the Encyclopaedia of the Philosophical Sciences), trans. William Wallace and A. C. Miller (Oxford: Clarendon Press, 1971), p. 143 (§410).

7 C. S. Peirce, 'How to Make Our Ideas Clear', in *The Essential Peirce: Selected Philosophical Writings*, ed. Nathan Houser and Christian J. W. Kloesel (Bloomington: Indiana University Press, 1992), p. 129.

8 See John Dewey, *Human Nature and Conduct*, in *John Dewey: The Middle Works, 1899–1924*, ed. Jo Ann Boydston (Carbondale: Southern Illinois University Press, 1988), p. 21; Gilles Deleuze, *Empiricism and Subjectivity*, trans. Constantin V. Boundas (New York: Columbia University Press, 1991).

9 Maine de Biran, *The Influence of Habit on the Faculty of Thinking*, trans. Margaret Donaldson Boehm (Westport, CT: Greenwood Press, 1970), p. 47.

10 Maine de Biran, *The Influence of Habit on the Faculty of Thinking*, pp. 47–48.

11 Kierkegaard, *Works of Love*, trans. Howard V. Hong and Edna H. Hong (Princeton: Princeton University Press, 1998), p. 36.

Made in the USA
San Bernardino, CA
30 June 2020